DEFI

DECENTRALIZED

FINANCE

INVESTING

2022

AND BEYOND

"An investment in knowledge pays the best interest"

- Benjamin Franklin.

GET A FREE AUDIOBOOK

EMAIL SUBJECT LINE:

"DEFI 2022"

TO

MINDSETMASTERSHIP@GMAIL.COM

JOIN OUR

NFT, CRYPTO ART,

METAVERSE & DEFI

Entrepreneur Power Group

To help reinforce the learning's from our books, I strongly suggest you join our well-informed powerhouse community on Facebook.

Here, you will connect and share with other like-minded people to support your journey and help you grow.

>>>CLICK BELOW to join Our NFT Group <<<

News Site & Community Group:

https://www.facebook.com/groups/nfttrending/

Want Future Book Releases?

Email us at:

mindsetmastership@gmail.com

Find us on Instagram!

@MindsetMastership

MASTERSHIP BOOKS

UK | USA | Canada | Ireland | Australia

India | New Zealand | South Africa | China

Mastership Books is part of the United Arts Publishing House group of companies based in London, England, UK.

First published by Mastership Books (London, UK), 2022

I S B N: 978-1-915002-24-2

Colour separation by Spitting Image Design Studio

Printed and bound in Great Britain

National Publications Association of Britain

London, England, United Kingdom.

Paper design UAP

ISBN: 978-1-915002-24-2

(paperback)

A723.5

Title: **Metaverse Investing Ultimate Guide**

Design, Bound & Printed:

London, England,

Great Britain.

*"If you really want to invest in something today, start investing your knowledge in **NFTs**, **Metaverse** and **DeFi**, these hidden treasure are going mainstream"*

CONTENTS

INTRODUCTION

Evolution of DeFi

Decentralized Finance (DeFi) is a category of blockchain-based solutions that tries to address the issues with traditional Finance, such as centralization and a lack of personal autonomy and control over one's funds. You can study the development of this new financial system under two distinct phases, DeFi 1.0 and DeFi 2.0. Let's begin by understanding the concept and features of these two editions and how their reinvention simplifies and improve the decentralized finance ecosystem.

DeFi 1.0

This is the first generation of the decentralized finance system. It includes a wide range of financial services, including decentralized exchanges (DEXes), yield farming or liquidity providing, governance for decentralized autonomous organizations (DAOs), lending platforms, payment gateways, etc.

DeFi 2.0

DeFi 2.0 is the second generation of DeFi protocols, and it tries to address the issues that plagued the earlier version.

Comparing DeFi 1.0 and 2.0

DeFi 1.0

The first issue is the risk of embracing new technologies. A lot can go wrong with DeFi 1.0. Individual cryptocurrency volatility has implications in DeFi since price movements might result in a temporary loss for liquidity providers (LP).

If someone steals your cash or hacks your smart contracts, there is nothing you can do because no single individual is held responsible for security breaches on decentralized platforms. Today, many users put their money into smart contracts without comprehending the possibility of loss. Because cryptocurrencies exist on multiple blockchains, less popular platforms suffer from low or inconsistent liquidity, and their related currencies are not always readily traded. Users may need to use numerous platforms to trade assets with limited liquidity or suffer losses due to slippage.

DeFi 2.0

DeFi 2.0 is a risk-reduction strategy. You can use impermanent loss insurance to compensate for an impermanent loss. Smart contracts, likewise, can be covered by smart contract insurance. Security audits conducted by open-source communities or insurance companies guarantee that smart contracts do not have serious weaknesses or exploitable back doors. Cross-chain bridges, which connect blockchains through layers of smart contracts and liquidity pools, can compensate for low liquidity by allowing users access to assets that aren't native to the blockchain. If an asset doesn't have enough liquidity on one chain, it can trade across good pools on other networks.

DeFi 2.0 may mitigate both DeFi 1.0 and traditional finance concerns, giving it an economic paradigm unlike anything seen before in the markets. Loan in DeFi 1.0, for example, is similar to traditional lending procedures but on a peer-to-peer basis. Users borrow money from other users at a high-interest rate, generally in exchange for a large quantity of collateral. Loans can, however, reimburse themselves in DeFi 2.0. Self-repaying loans employ collateral for yield farming (liquidity provision that reinvests yield) to pay off the loan debt. The borrower gets their original collateral after a passive income stream has repaid the whole sum, and they have effectively paid nothing out of pocket.

The second key issue that each new technology faces are accessibility. While everyone now has access to the internet, only a few individuals had access to the computers required to use it at first. The adoption of cryptocurrency and DeFi 1.0 both ran into the same issue. For a decade, the bitcoin industry was a closed sector dominated by people who used language to appear intelligent. Buzzwords like distributed ledger technology, fungibility, etc., might convince fellow crypto fans that you are not entirely ignorant and aware of the current trends.

DeFi 2.0 aims to educate and integrate individuals into the current system. By updating its story over time, cryptocurrency figured out how to make itself accessible to the average person, and it's now a household issue. DeFi 2.0 uses this approach, and it aims to make DeFi accessible to everyone through two primary ideas: education and interaction with established financial systems. The most successful DeFi 2.0 projects have streamlined front-end functionality and generated resources to teach new users about their platform. When it comes to DeFi, which is fundamentally decentralized, integration with centralized, traditional banking networks is a contentious topic. Traditional financial institutions may integrate DeFi 2.0 protocols into their platforms via APIs and oracles, which connect blockchains to other systems, as DeFi 2.0 becomes more accessible.

Layers 1 and 2 in the DeFi Ecosystem

We can attribute DeFi's allure and appeal to its structural integrity and functional adaptability, distinguishing Layer 1 and Layer 2.

The decentralized finance ecosystem is exceedingly complicated and growing quickly. To have a functional model for any service in DeFi requires a complex structure of components that includes cutting-edge programming in blockchain technology and a keen understanding of financial economics. Devastating losses or network breakdowns might come from a single miscalculation in either the programming or financial aspects.

As a result, DeFi is set up to aid the prevention of market-wide problems. The idea that you can stack all projects on top of one other or function in parallel is decentralized, much like DeFi. Layer 1 and Layer 2 solutions are terminologies used in DeFi to describe this stacking. But what exactly is a Layer 1 solution, and how is it different from a Layer 2 solution?

We can divide almost all blockchains and services in the DeFi network into two layers: Layer 1 and Layer 2, and we are now on the verge of Layer 3 protocols.

Layer 1 Blockchain Solutions

Layer 1 solutions are the essential and foundational operating pieces of the network in the DeFi ecosystem. These are the pillar structures from which the entire ecosystem benefits directly and may communicate. As a result, these structures also assist in maintaining integrity for other projects, allowing them to perform more complex applications that would otherwise be impossible.

Amazon delivery, for example, would be impossible to achieve without the infrastructure of housing, towns, transportation, and logistics. Layer 1 solutions make up the network's foundational system, and layer 1 protocols can be piled on top of one other to help projects succeed.

Ethereum, Polkadot, Cosmos, Binance Smart Chain, Band Protocol, Solana, and Nervous Network are the most popular Layer 1 solutions. Layer 1 is also applicable to Bitcoin. Ethereum, Polkadot, and Binance Smart Chain are examples of blockchains that help build the foundations for the whole ecosystem. Ethereum, for example, is the first and largest blockchain to support smart connections, allowing companies to function on top of Ethereum while focusing on creating complex applications.

In this sense, Ethereum smart contracts allow projects such as Aave and Compound by establishing the ERC-20 token standard. Because of Ethereum, applications like Uniswap, Sushiswap, Balancer, and NFTs are feasible. Those and other projects like Balancer and Compound are built on Ethereum's Layer 1 solution.

Layer 2 Blockchain Solutions

Layer 1's fundamentals and the advantages they provided aided in creating Layer 2 protocols. Layer 2 blockchain solutions are blockchain functional components built on top of the foundation provided by Layer 1.

Layer 2 solutions include custodial services, vendor deliveries, and modern transportation that the city inherits, in the case of the city economy, where Layer 1 is businesses and roadways. The opportunity to design something more complex because of the absence of the need to recreate the core characteristics that Layer 1 currently provides is a significant benefit of Layer 2 solutions. Furthermore, Layer 2 solutions can immediately benefit from Layer 1 efforts to improve the ecosystem.

For example, we've demonstrated that blockchains like Ethereum, Polkadot, and Binance Smart Chain are all Layer 1 solutions. Ethereum allows projects like Compound and Balancer to exist using Uniswap. The main disadvantage of these projects is that they can only exist and function well if Layer 1 projects are working correctly. Layer 2 projects would be bankrupt if something hampered the ETH chain, such as gas congestion or an issue with ERC-20 compatibility.

How Can DeFi Go Mainstream

We are about to witness a huge increase in institutional credit flow into the digital economy. In 2022, DeFi will become popular, knowledge will grow, institutional opinion will continue to favor cryptocurrency, and the DeFi strengths will grow. Faster, more capital-efficient, and compliant services will result from this acceptance, which will benefit both the digital and real-world economies.

DAOs (Decentralized Autonomous Organizations)

In 2022, institutions will not be the only ones who benefit. To diversify treasuries and reward their communities, crypto-native DAOs will increase investments. Family offices, wealth managers, and venture capital firms will continue investing and expanding. Everyone wants a slice of the DeFi pie, and there's plenty to go around.

Ethereum 2.0

We anticipate that when Ethereum switches to PoS (Proof of Stake), the lower transaction costs on Layer 1 will cement Ethereum's position as the preferred platform for DeFi apps. Furthermore, because the environmental concern will no longer be relevant, the shift in consensus-mechanism may open the door to other kinds of money.

Layer 2 Scaling Protocols

We began to see some Layer 2 usage in 2021. However, transaction costs are still greater than sidechains, and their ecosystem is still in its infancy. We anticipate that in 2022, CEXs' (centralized exchanges) Layer 2 deposit/withdrawal capability and the availability of bridge protocols will significantly improve the Layer 2 user experience.

Interoperability and the Evolution of Multichain Cryptocurrency

By default, the first multichain apps, which utilize numerous Layer 1 as part of their core protocol, will appear in 2022. We will witness an ecosystem of multiple blockchains functioning together as other new chains join the field.

Cosmos and Polkadot, both multichain ecosystems, can offer us an idea of what this means. Both employ similar structures, including a central 'hub' and specialized blockchains built on the protocol that links to it. The benefit is that interoperability across various chains is achieved at the protocol level, allowing each chain to be tailored to unique use cases while maintaining the same level of security.

Layer 2 protocols

To offset Ethereum's high fees and delayed scaling solutions, the popularity of Layer 1 chains and sidechains has skyrocketed in 2022. However, 2022 will be when Layer 2 Ethereum achieves critical mass acceptance, surpassing Layer 1 in terms of both TVL [total value locked] and volume.

Myths About DeFi

As decentralized finance grows in popularity, it's important to consider some common myths about the technology.

Anonymity

Digital currencies may be generated, traded, and controlled on the blockchain using decentralized financial systems. This implies that instead of being monitored by a single, centralized bank, everything inside the ecosystem is shared and synced among various computer nodes that validate transactions. To open an account or exchange currencies, customers do not need to submit verification of their identities, giving the system an initial level of anonymity not previously possible with most financial institutions.

However, being a distributed ledger, the blockchain keeps track of every transaction on its network. Furthermore, anyone with access to the system may see these transactions. While users may not be required to disclose personal information to join the system, transactions they conduct are easily traceable. Following these transactions back to a bank account where the monies are placed, government or law enforcement organizations can trace the trail to a specific person.

The fundamental objective of blockchain technology enabling decentralized financial systems is to help millions of unique nodes that verify every transaction and communicate that information publicly, ensuring that the system is accurate. Because of this procedure, while individual transactions may not reveal a person's identity, they leave a trail that hinders total anonymity.

Elimination of Personal Risk

There is also a prevalent myth that decentralized finance is intrinsically safer than centralized systems managed by a single financial institution. The blockchain employs many different sources to verify and record what happens inside the system.

While the blockchain helps protect against administrative or accounting errors — as one family recently discovered when they got $50 billion in their account by mistake — it also removes the precautions that centralized financial firms give. The majority of today's most powerful financial firms have existed for decades, and federal and industry regulations have been put in place to protect against fraud. These measures might be difficult to navigate, but they provide essential protection. On the other side, with many DeFi systems, a person's sole protection is the unique login credentials they need to access their account. In certain circumstances, all that's required is a username and password. If hackers gain access to this data, they will be able to wipe away a victim's entire amount in seconds. Unfortunately, this is what happened with the cryptocurrency exchange Coinbase lately, leaving victims with no way of retrieving their stolen assets and no industry oversight to assist.

DeFi Adoption Means the End of Banks

When decentralized finance systems gained traction in the late 2010s, enthusiasts and financial sector professionals speculated that the technology may mean the end for many of the world's big financial institutions. Digital monies would eventually replace national currencies, and smart contracts on the blockchain would give traditional institutions better and more secure access to lending, investing, and even real estate transactions. Even the International Monetary Fund published a report that looked into the possibility of DeFi being the new global standard.

The truth is a little more complicated. While banks may risk becoming an industry relic if they choose to remain on the sidelines while these developments occur, this is highly improbable. Although the business is expanding more slowly than others, a few financial institutions are already investing heavily in cryptocurrencies and associated services. It's also worth noting that, while DeFi services were among the first to use blockchain's smart contracts, the technology isn't limited to bitcoin. For example, Barclays in the United Kingdom is already collaborating with a company called Wave to utilize smart contracts to improve payment procedures, opening the path for further cooperation in the future.

Decentralized finance has increased in popularity in recent years, and for a good reason. However, while cryptocurrencies and the underlying blockchain technology are delivering significant new services for individual customers and substantial financial organizations, we must differentiate between fiction and truth when it comes to these services.

Pros and Cons of DeFi

Pros of DeFi

Permissionless

The term 'decentralized' is the first and most crucial aspect that determines the identity of decentralized finance. One of the fundamental ideas of blockchain is decentralization, which helps to reduce reliance on businesses. Decentralized finance also relieves the burden of relying on institutions for monitoring, data storage, server space, and other considerations. Blockchain networks effectively achieve these qualities by ensuring that individual transaction records are disseminated among all users.

The decentralization benefits banking and finance democratization. DeFi may provide everyone with easy and efficient access to financial services. The bulk of DeFi solutions operate on Ethereum, and Ethereum is the second-largest blockchain system, and it is highly decentralized due to its permissionless nature.

The permissionless characteristics of blockchain in DeFi apps may potentially benefit from blockchain's interoperability support. As a result, it may provide a variety of configurable alternatives for third-party integrations. At the same time, it's important to note that Ethereum's permissionless blockchain capabilities aren't unique. Ethereum is a reliable alternative for constructing DeFi apps since it is a favored network for developing smart contracts.

Immutability

Blockchain has achieved true immutability thanks to successful encryption and consensus techniques such as proof-of-work. As a result, the advantages and drawbacks of decentralized finance have permitted real immutability in the finance industry.

Thanks to immutability, it isn't easy to modify any record on the blockchain network. In addition to the benefits of decentralization, immutability provides a reasonable security assurance. Surprisingly, the blockchain's immutability features safeguard the integrity of DeFi systems when conducting financial transactions.

Transparency

While immutability is a crucial necessity for the DeFi landscape to assure security, transparency is one of the significant contributions among DeFi professionals. Decentralization means more clarity, and the distributed ledger keeps track of everything on the blockchain network.

The cryptographic principles of blockchain also ensure that information is only documented when verified as valid. The benefits and drawbacks of DeFi highlight how users may benefit from DeFi apps' transparency.

With transparency, DeFi applications may help users recognize and avoid potential financial frauds and bad business practices. DeFi applications might simplify the determination of individuals who made modifications to a transaction, when they happened, and how they happened with a clear audit trail. As a result, little would be left to jeopardize the financial ecosystem's integrity.

Applications for Lending and Borrowing

DeFi has also played an essential role in the growth of peer-to-peer lending and borrowing solutions. End-users can profit significantly from these forms of lending and borrowing options. The benefits and drawbacks of decentralized finance will undoubtedly affect the cryptographic verification process.

They also give the certainty of smart contract integration at the same time. The availability of such features removes the need for intermediaries like banks, which are typically in charge of verifying the participants of a transaction. You can use it to verify the processes involved in lending and borrowing. As a result, DeFi makes the verification method for lending and borrowing applications faster and easier. DeFi also guarantees that counterparties in a transaction are protected. DeFi lending apps would also enable the advantages of faster transaction resolution and improved accessibility.

Lending and borrowing applications are now the most well-known DeFi applications. Compound is one of the notable examples of DeFi lending and borrowing platforms. It's a decentralized lending platform that allows lenders to transfer crypto assets to a collection of lending pools. Other individuals can borrow from the lending pools, and lenders will get a percentage of the interest paid back by borrowers. We can determine a lender's interest rate by the amount of money they provide to the pool. Furthermore, the liquidity of crypto-assets has a significant impact on the internet rate on DeFi lending services.

Savings Applications

DeFi might help people manage their funds more effectively, and users may begin earning interest on assets locked in lending protocols such as Compound. As a result, many DeFi-based savings apps have popped up in recent years. Such apps allow users to tap into numerous loan protocols to increase their earning potential.

Tokenization

Discussions on pros and cons of DeFi would be incomplete without mentioning the benefits of tokenization. Tokenization is one of the most talked-about concepts in the blockchain world, and Ethereum provides extensive smart contract capabilities, paving the way for crypto token issuance.

Crypto tokens functioned as digital assets on a blockchain with various functions and applications. Tokens include utility tokens that are exclusive to a particular dApp, real estate tokens, and security tokens, to name a few. Tokens can help you achieve many functions. Real estate tokens may assist you in attaining fractional ownership of tangible assets. On the other hand, you can use security tokens as digital shares in specialized applications. Summarily, tokenization may allow greater exposure to other real and digital assets.

Digital currencies, fiat currencies, oil, and gold are all possible assets. Tokens in Ethereum-based smart contracts serve as collateral for crypto-synthetic assets. Synthetix, one of the largest synthetic asset platforms, now has roughly $600 million locked in its smart contracts.

Cons of Decentralized Finance

Scalability

DeFi apps are unquestionably appropriate for facilitating financial inclusion for a larger audience. However, DeFi projects have significant challenges in the scalability of the host blockchain from many angles. First and foremost, DeFi transactions need an extraordinarily long confirmation period. At the same time, transactions over DeFi protocols may become prohibitively costly during periods of congestion. For example, with Ethereum at maximum capacity, it could execute around 13 transactions per second. On the other hand, DeFi's centralized equivalents could handle thousands of transactions simultaneously.

Uncertainty

If a blockchain hosting a DeFi project becomes unstable, the project may inherit the instability from the host blockchain. The Ethereum blockchain is currently undergoing several improvements, and mistakes made during the transfer from PoW to Eth 2.0 PoS, for example, might result in uncertainties.

Liquidity Concerns

In DeFi-based applications and blockchain technologies, liquidity is unquestionably essential. The overall value locked in DeFi projects is more than $12.5 billion as of October 2020. As a result, the DeFi market is smaller than traditional banking systems. Hence, putting your faith in a sector that lacks the resources of the traditional financial industry might be challenging.

Shared Responsibility

Among all DeFi's drawbacks, the shared responsibility is negative for users. The DeFi projects are not linked to your errors, and all they do is remove the intermediaries, leaving the users accountable for their finances and assets. As a result, the DeFi space needs solutions to avoid human errors and blunders.

Role of Smart Contract in DeFi Development

Smart contracts, which have increased the popularity of DeFi smart contract development, propel DeFi technologies. The smart contract is used because it helps both businesses and users. Smart contract development for DeFi is creating, auditing, and implementing a smart contract that automatically delivers decentralized finance services without a central authority. It shortens the time to complete decentralized financial transactions, including lending, investing, insurance, and banking.

Smart contracts are pre-defined automated code lines that a buyer and seller agree to for certain activities. You can execute the contract's functions when the smart contract's pre-defined criteria are satisfied. Many service providers, including smart contract development and audits, provide smart contract creation as a stand-alone solution for decentralized finance services.

Centralized financial organizations can become decentralized through the use of smart contracts. By making financial organizations decentralized, it overcomes the following issues.

- Inadequate digitalization. Traditional financial institutions only offer a small number of internet-based services. As a result, it doesn't appeal to the next generation of users. Bank decentralization, however, can save 60-80% of expenditures.
- Security concerns. Security is important when it comes to financing. Customers are concerned about frequent financial service outages as well as security breaches. Because the system

is based on Blockchain, no single person or group of individuals can control the design.

- Extraneous Factors. External factors that impact a financial organization's success include natural disasters, government regulations, and competition. Decentralization makes it possible to check all these factors.
- Conflict in traditional financial systems. Traditional banking is prone to buyer-seller conflicts due to its centralized nature. Constantly changing regulations, fraudulent operations, and lacking organizational resources contribute to conflict.
- High transaction fee. You can keep transaction fees at a minimum because smart contract-based DeFi protocols do not rely on third parties.
- The absence of human interference. For speed, the entire procedure is automated. As a result, physical work is almost non-existent, and performance exceeds that of traditional services.

DeFi Uses Cases in 2022

Examples of DeFi use cases currently seen in 2022 are:

Payment Networks and Remittances Across the Country

El Salvador developed a Bitcoin and Lightning-based payment network in September 2021 to handle both inward remittance payments and point-of-sale payments. Various independent service providers and banks put up the service in a couple of months to provide wallet apps (like Chivo and Strike) and gateways to the Bitcoin and Lightning networks, all based on open-source components.

There are three driving forces behind this initiative:

- Remittances are less expensive. El Salvador derives its GDP from overseas to 25% (mainly from the USA). This usually involves paying a 5-10% charge to the regular banking system.

- Inclusion in the financial system. Even the weakest members of society have benefited from the shift from cash to digital payments.
- El Salvador is the world's first country to make Bitcoin legal tender. El Salvadorean merchants have upgraded their cash register software. Users may now choose to keep their wallet balance in US dollars or Bitcoin and swap back and forth between the two with ease, limiting their exposure to volatility. A government fund is used to provide liquidity.

Acceptance by the Merchant

Bitpay is one of the first merchants to allow crypto payment platforms. Buyers can pick crypto as a payment option during a fiat check-out. Bitpay's services calculate the equivalent amount in crypto in real-time and present it to the user. The customer makes a payment (for example, scanning a QR code using a wallet app), and the merchant verifies the transaction. Bitpay usually sends the money to the merchant in fiat currency.

Regal Group (an operator of 500 theaters in the United States) stated in November 2021 that they would start accepting digital tokens for purchasing movie tickets, snacks, and refreshments. Regal uses the Layer 2 Flexa network to let users spend various cryptocurrencies, stablecoins, and digital tokens straight from their wallet applications (including Bitcoin, Ethereum, Dogecoin, Litecoin, etc. GeminiDollar, DAI, Link, Atom, and BAT). The transaction is paid instantaneously once the user scans a bar code presented at the cash register. Regal is paid in fiat currencies through Flexa's regulated section.

B2B Payments

DeFi provides a plethora of alternatives for forward-thinking treasurers. Thanks to an increasing number of licensed exchanges, they can use, keep, and transfer stable currency values quickly and cheaply. There are no negative interest rates in effect. More daring treasurers, such as

Michael Saylor's listed business MicroStrategy, are betting big on non-fiat crypto. MicroStrategy changed all of its spare cash into Bitcoin in the summer of 2020, a massive event in the crypto and DeFi ecosystems. Tesla and Square are among the corporations that have followed suit since then.

DeFi promises quicker, better, and less expensive payments, but there are a lot of roadblocks to overcome, including legislative, commercial, and technical acceptance of this new infrastructure. Nonetheless, incumbent financial institutions benefit from this change since they already have services and customers looking for lower prices and improved quality. A 'behind-the-scenes' infrastructure upgrade does not have to disrupt the essential user experience, as voice over IP (VoIP) proved a few decades ago; it improves the service by enhancing the quality and lowering costs. DeFi might achieve a similar result behind-the-scenes, with today's market infrastructure gradually moving to this more decentralized technological stack.

Factors Driving the Growth of DeFi

Decentralized Finance is flourishing, with total value locked rising from $700 million in December 2019 to more than $200 billion by 2022, almost equal to Greece's 2017 GDP. Accessibility, convenience of usage, and yields are the three key factors driving DeFi's development.

System Openness

One of the initial aims of crypto and DeFi is to promote financial inclusion by ensuring that the 1.7 billion people without an active bank account have access to the same benefits as those who use traditional finance, such as paying bills, getting insurance, and building a pension pot.

To achieve this, blockchain technology has been created so that everyone with a smartphone may use it. With 91 percent of people possessing a smartphone, this design has given thousands of individuals who were previously termed "unbanked" access to financial services. In nations where switching currencies is difficult, like Venezuela, it has also allowed people to preserve their savings from inflation by trading fiat for cryptocurrency.

The Ease of Usage

DeFi has sparked a lot of interest because it is simple to use and opens the door to millions of 'unbanked' individuals. People see Crypto and DeFi as a scary industry reserved only for the tech-savvy. Things have changed, and several platforms, such as AQRU, now allow investors to convert their fiat cash into cryptocurrency and reap the vast profits available in DeFi.

While these platforms were initially designed for retail investors, new solutions are being developed to allow institutional investors to easily access the decentralized market, maintain tight control over their investments, and remain compliant with any relevant regulatory and security requirements.

Sky-high Returns

The yields are one of the most tempting aspects of decentralized Finance for investors. There are no middlemen between transactions in DeFi; everything is done peer-to-peer. The lender can collect practically all of the yield by removing all intermediate procedures.

Let's take a look at a bank as an example. If consumers are lucky, a savings account with a bank will yield 0.5 percent each year. The bank may have made a 10% profit by lending money to clients, but by the time they've covered their costs and taken their cut, there's not much left for the customer. The upkeep of DeFi's website, which has attracted users trying to maximize their profits, is its major cost.

CHAPTER 1

THE DEFI ECOSYSTEM TRENDS

T he bitcoin and blockchain industries had a fantastic year in 2021. In 2021, cryptocurrencies such as Bitcoin and Ethereum reached fresh all-time highs. According to Wind's statistics, Bitcoin is the top-performing main asset and alternative asset in 2021, with a growth rate of 72 percent from the beginning to the end of the year, exceeding crude oil and natural gas. Bitcoin is only one example of how digital assets change the financial industry. The asset's success attracted increased attention to the crypto and blockchain industries, leading to a surge in users and cash inflows.

With the number of new protocols increasing and established ones consolidating their positions, Web 3.0 and other novel solutions that may absorb DeFi space and make it more available to a new audience of users will emerge in 2022. Various protocols implemented DAOs throughout 2021, and many influencers backed their implementation. Although not all DAOs were successful, their core operating ideas are strong enough to be utilized as the basis for forming legal companies.

With the Ethereum London upgrade, TVL on Layer 1 vs Layer 2, node distribution for leading blockchains, gas utilization, and so on, 2021 witnessed many changes in the blockchain ecosystem, which is expected to enter 2022. BSC, Avalanche, and Solana are all lagging behind Ethereum TVL. There are new solutions to improve network usage comfort while reducing gas fees. In 2022, the Ethereum network will continue to scale, introduce updates, and adopt rivals like Solana as industry anchors.

The BTC and ETH networks have seen the most growth and performance of cross-chain bridges, which have become passive tools due to low development traction and other inefficiencies. We expect similar advancement rates on cross-chain development in 2022 and widespread adoption of such solutions logically across significant ecosystems. We expect the focus on Layer 1 and decentralized finance to continue throughout 2022. There's still a lot of room for improvement, whether in terms of Layer 1 scalability or more sophisticated and rewarding DeFi protocols. The following are some more trends to keep an eye on:

NFTs

GameFi

DAOs

SocialFi

MetaFi

Regulation

The Best DeFi Platforms in 2022

In this section, we have summarized a list of key categories of DeFi platforms with examples and their distinguishing features to guide your choice and investment decisions

DeFi Lending Platforms

One of the most significant advantages of DeFi lending platforms is that, unlike banks and other centralized lending choices, you may earn interest and incentives every minute instead of once a month by lending out bitcoins (often stablecoins). By pledging their crypto holdings as collateral, crypto-financing allows investors to borrow assets in cash or crypto. When employing crypto lending, the lender keeps ownership of the digital asset. However, we can not relocate the coin provided as collateral throughout the loan period.

The procedure for using these platforms is pretty simple:

- A user loans cryptocurrency to a platform, usually stablecoins, without filling out any documentation. By doing so, they earn interest.
- A borrower contacts the bitcoin lending site and inquires about obtaining a loan.
- The borrower's cryptocurrency secures the loan, and the platform accepts the loan and attaches the collateral. Before a borrower gets their money, they must repay the entire amount.
- The site will liquidate the user's debt into stablecoins if collateral falls below a specific threshold. We do this to keep the collateral's value higher than the loan's.

Aave (Token: $AAVE)

The Aave protocol is a non-custodial, decentralized liquidity platform built on Ethereum. It allows users to supply and borrow crypto assets while returning the support they contribute to the protocol. In reaction to supply and demand in the protocol, the yield on any crypto assets issued varies dynamically and algorithmically. You may connect to the Aave protocol using any other 100+ integrated onramps to get started. Access aave.com or app.aave.com to see which assets are supported.

Aave's total value locked (TVL) is 18.44 billion dollars. It's recognized as one of the greatest lending protocols and one of the most secure DeFi systems, having undergone many third-party audits and testing. It receives a 95 Security Score from Certik.

Maker (Token: $MKR)

MakerDAO is a decentralized credit network based on Ethereum that releases Dai, a USD-pegged stablecoin. Maker allows anybody to open a Vault, deposit ETH, BAT, USDC, or other acceptable assets as collateral, and produce Dai as debt. You assess and pay a stability fee (i.e., the loan's interest) upon the return of borrowed Dai on Dai debt.

MKR is Maker's second token, and holders have the power to vote on system governance concerns such as altering the stability charge and other risk criteria. If a black swan event happens, these token holders will have the last say on whether or not to intervene. Maker has a TVL of 15.74 billion dollars. It is regarded as a highly secure platform, with an 85 Security Score, making it one of the top DeFi lending protocols and one of the most significant Aave rivals.

InstaDApp (Token: $INST)

Built on popular DeFi projects like MakerDAO, Compound, Uniswap, and others, Instadapp is a smart wallet with a simple UI for managing assets. It's made easy to use regardless of the user's technical or financial background. The dashboard allows users to see all their DeFi positions in one location.

The community now controls the Instadapp protocol thanks to INST, Instadapp's governance token, launched in 2021. Token holders handle the platform's underlying contracts and future upgrades. The market capitalization of Instadapp is 12.5 billion dollars. Although the project still lacks an official security rating, it has been subjected to public audits by other parties.

Compound Finance. ($COMP)

Users may earn interest or borrow assets in return for collateral using Compound, an Ethereum-based algorithmic money market system. Anyone may add assets to Compound's liquidity pool and immediately earn compound interest. Rates are adjusted automatically based on user traffic.

cTokens are representations of the asset that produce interest and act as security for asset balances that have been delivered. Users can borrow between 50% and 75% of their cTokens (depending on the perceived quality of the underlying asset). Funds can be added or removed, but if the debt becomes undercollateralized, others can liquidate it; liquidators get a 5% discount on liquidated assets as an incentive.

The TVL of Compound is 11.48 billion dollars. A security score of 95 is considered one of the most secure DeFi systems.

Liquity ($LQTY)

Liquity is an interest-free, collateralized borrowing system with innovative, immediately batched liquidations on stablecoin. It has no governance (fully unchangeable), and its minimum collateral ratio is only 110 percent. A certain amount of ETH is placed as collateral (with a modest percentage charge) to issue an amount of the LUSD stablecoin to construct a "Trove" (a collateralized debt position). LUSD can be put in the Stability Pool when troves are liquidated and utilized to regulate supply and demand, earning part of the liquidated ETH.

Liquity has a TVL of 2.11 billion dollars, making it a decent alternative for lending and borrowing. According to third-party audits, it has a 96 percent Security Score. As a result, it is also one of the most relevant Aave rivals.

DEXs (Decentralized Exchanges)

A decentralized exchange (or DEX) is a platform that allows cryptocurrency traders to deal with one another directly (peer-to-peer). DEXs facilitate financial transactions that aren't handled by banks, brokers, or other third parties, which is one of crypto's most crucial aspects. Several large DEXs, notably Uniswap and Sushiwap, leverage the Ethereum blockchain. Unlike centralized exchanges such as Coinbase, DEXs do not allow for fiat-to-crypto conversions; instead, they only enable users to trade cryptocurrency tokens for cryptocurrency tokens. You need a controlled exchange (or CEX) to swap fiat for crypto or vice versa.

DEXs come in different shapes and sizes. The most well-known are:

Curve Finance (Token: $CRV)

Curve.fi is a well-known yTokens integrator that generates lending and trading fees by constructing an AMM between yUSDC, yDAI, yTUSD, and yUSDT. They act as a decentralized exchange liquidity pool that runs on the Ethereum network, allowing optimal stablecoin trading and lending with minimal slippage and costs.

There are hundreds of Curve pools, the most popular of which are trycrypto2, steth, lusd, mim, Y, ren, and 3pool, which conduct swaps for a range of stablecoins and assets. Curve has a TVL of $14.4 billion, and Curve has had at least three public third-party audits.

Uniswap (Token: $UNI)

Uniswap is an Ethereum token exchange that uses liquidity pools rather than order books to trade tokens. Anyone may simply convert ETH to any ERC20 token or earn fees by providing any level of liquidity. Similarly, anyone can establish a liquidity pool by donating an equivalent quantity of their token and ETH. More than one market for the same token is not permitted. Once a market creator creates an exchange rate, it will begin to vary according to the "constant product market maker" process used by Uniswap. The price changes as a trade reduce one side of the pair's liquidity relative to the other. Arbitrage is encouraged by this process, which promotes trade and overall liquidity.

On Uniswap, liquidity pairings do not have unique tokens issued to them. Instead, it represents each liquidity pair with a unique and readily transferable ERC20 token. At least five public third-party audits have been performed on Uniswap. It has a TVL of $7.43 billion.

SushiSwap (Token: $SUSHI)

Sushiswap is a decentralized on-chain token exchange technology that employs automated market-making (AMM) and uses 'liquidity pools' rather than order books. You can use its token ($SUSHI) to distribute user transaction fees and grant voting rights on platform governance problems.

Uniswap and SushiSwap are identical, except that SUSHI offers a few unique features, such as a yield farming platform (we will discuss this in detail in a later chapter) and token-holder benefits. At the same time, UNI has a more significant trade volume and has been in operation for longer. The parallels aren't coincidental: SushiSwap is a fork of Uniswap's code with minor changes. The UI is inspired by a sushi menu and includes fun gaming features.

SUSHI was established in August 2020 by "Chef Nomi" (whose identity is unknown). It produced a lot of controversy between him and Uniswap's developer Hayden Adams, who was upset about billions of dollars in staked liquidity being "taken" by a simple replica of his idea shortly after introduction.

Sushiswap has a TVL of $4.57 billion, making it a decent option for users.

Balancer (Token: $BAL)

Balancer is an "n-dimensional automated market-maker" that works on Ethereum. Rather than a single ETH-token pair, several tokens make up its pool with changeable weights and trading fees instead of "traditional" AAM models. ETFs are an intriguing analogy: consumers establish preferred importance for the assets in their portfolio, and traders, not fund managers, constantly adjust it in search of arbitrage opportunities.

The Balancer protocol provides a lot of flexibility and allows for a few different pool configurations:

- Only a private pool owner may change the specifications and inject liquidity.
- Shared Pools, no one, not even the author, may modify the parameters.
- Any user can inject liquidity, and it uses a unique token called the Balancer Pool Token to keep track of liquidity shares (BPT).

Balancer receives a 6.35 security score from Cer.live, and the protocol's TLV is around $2 billion.

DeFi Payments Platforms

DeFi ecosystem also includes payment systems with unique features oriented toward efficiency or additional benefits. The following are some of the most well-known DeFi payment platforms:

Flexa

Flexa's digital network eliminates chargebacks and unexpected reversals, restoring merchant trust. It guarantees all payments from the moment they arrive at a POS. It connects directly to current payment infrastructures by partnering with various processors, middleware providers, and cloud POS. Because Flexa payments are digital, they are swift and safe. It uses digital authorization codes and an account balance model that converts currencies as needed.

Tornado Cash

Tornado Cash is a decentralized, Ethereum-based system that allows for private transactions. Promoting transaction privacy breaks the relationship between the source and destination blockchain addresses.

It uses a smart contract to accept ETH deposits that you can withdraw from different addresses. To ensure security, you can use a relayer to withdraw to an address with a 0 ETH balance. When ETH is withdrawn from a new address, there is no way to trace the withdrawal to the deposit in Tornado, ensuring perfect privacy.

The Tornado Cash protocol is decentralized and community-owned: neither the Tornado Cash founders nor any Tornado Cash servers influence it.

DeFi Asset Management Platforms

DeFi also provides solutions for customers to manage their assets, such as improving their value or facilitating access to complicated financial instruments. The following are some of the most often used asset management platforms in DeFi:

Convex Finance (Token: $CVX)

Convex Finance enables Curve.fi liquidity providers to earn trading fees, enhanced CRV, and liquidity mining benefits with little effort and without locking any CRV. Consumers may stake Curve LP tokens using a highly user-friendly interface on the Convex Finance website.

TVL amounts to around $7.7 billion with a Security Score of 70%.

Yearn.Finance (Token: $YFI)

Yearn.finance is a platform that uses loan services like Aave, Compound, Dydx, and Fulcrum to increase token lending. When a user deposits tokens with yearn. Finance, they are converted to yTokens, which the platform regularly rebalances to determine which lending service is the most profitable (s).

As a genuinely decentralized protocol, you can make all improvements to the yearn.finance ecosystem via on-chain proposals and voting.

Although it has been the subject of multiple public third-party audits, it does not have an official Security Score. Its TVL is about $4.93 billion.

Integration of Metaverse and DeFi

In 2021, the NFT and metaverse markets took center stage. They combine with DeFi and the gaming sector to create an ecosystem that empowers consumers and gives them control over trades and distribution of digital assets. With the metaverse serving as the primary hub for NFT activity, 2022 will be a watershed year for introducing breakthrough solutions in decentralized user identification and deploying different supporting systems for complete integration with DeFi.

DeFi Market Trends in 2022

The DeFi sector has plummeted to $105 billion as of January 2022, after reaching an all-time high of $174 billion in mid-November 2021. The downward spiral continued as the macro narrative of interest rate rises to combat inflation made all investments, not just crypto, less appealing than the new and improved "risk-free" rate. ETH and EVM compatible networks outperformed other chains during the bear market, as decentralized apps incurred huge losses. Solana, for example, experienced many outages while being able to process more transactions per second than Ethereum. A rapid increase in computing transactions pressured Solana's network. DeFi wallet use grew this month despite the dip, with 4.3 million unique addresses. Even though individuals may have many wallets/addresses, this data point provides a valuable snapshot of the DeFi ecosystem's general health. Ethereum remains the most dominant chain despite the dip, accounting for over 60% of the Defi TVL.

Popular DeFi protocols' monthly income has dropped to roughly $280 million, around the same time last year. However, since December 2021, SpookySwap, a DEX for the Fantom Opera network, has quadrupled its income. Several lending regimes have seen a decline in deposits and loans for the month. The entire value of deposits for the three main lending procedures was $31.2 billion, down 26% on average from December. The total value of borrowing was $14.9 billion, down 23% on average from December. Since January 2021, the DeFi Pulse Index (DPI), a capitalization-weighted index that monitors DeFi's performance, has returned +61.4 percent, a year-to-date return of -36 percent.

Meanwhile, since January 2021, ETH has gained +246.7 percent and lost -30 percent year-to-date, exceeding both Bitcoin and the index. As capital continues to move throughout the Ethereum ecosystem, we track and evaluate the increase of DeFi wallets, TVL, and cumulative income, to name a few things. Millions of individuals use the Ethereum blockchain to develop and participate in a new economic system powered by code which is attributed to the growing activity and interest in the DeFi market. In 2021, there are a plethora of institutional DeFi milestones, indicating an "up only" trip of institutional interest in 2022 and a huge investment and profitable opportunities.

DeFi Creative Startups to Watch

Below is a list of top DeFi startups establishing themselves as leaders in the decentralized finance ecosystem.

Uniswap

Uniswap is one of the first decentralized financial companies, most known for its 400 UNI token airdrop (giveaway) to anybody who engaged with Uniswap or utilized the service. The token airdrop was worth $1200 at the time. Today, approximately $13,000. Uniswap is a decentralized system for trading on the Ethereum blockchain" that has processed over $209 billion in volume to date.

Yearn Finance

Founded in 2020, Yearn Finance is the go-to platform for "yield farmers," or those who seek arbitrage opportunities by supplying tokens as liquidity to other networks. Yearn allows a yield farmer to optimize income and rebalance automatically without performing the mental labor of switching from platform to platform and token to token.

Rocketpool

If you've ever heard of cryptocurrencies, you've probably heard the word "staking." Staking is using cryptocurrency to help protect the blockchain in exchange for incentives, interest, or tokens. Many people without coding experience think staking on the Ethereum blockchain is too technical, complex, and hazardous. This is where Rocketpool comes in. Rocketpool is a staking feature that allows users to stake with lower minimums than necessary, making the process more accessible.

AAVE

AAVE is a major participant in the DeFi industry. Users may lend crypto and receive aTokens at a 1:1 ratio, resulting in interest accumulating over time as the platform functions as a lending and borrowing marketplace. Users may also take out "flash loans," which are unsecured, uncollateralized loans that allow them to borrow and repay simultaneously.

Synthetix

Synthetix is the premier on-chain, secure derivatives trading platform in the DeFi industry, allowing users to stake SNX tokens. With almost $2 billion locked in the platform, it's gaining increasing attention. Gold, US dollars, and other assets are accessible in the Synthetix ecosystem.

Top DeFi Cryptos in 2022

Terra (LUNA)

Terra's price increased by about 13,000 percent in 2021, but it has since decreased in 2022, as with many other cryptos. It's a DeFi ecosystem based on algorithmic stablecoins, nicknamed the "next generation of money." Stablecoins will be used to create a fully digital financial system. Thousands of shops in Korea use Terra's Chai payment technology, and its Anchor savings program is gaining traction.

The value of stablecoin is linked to a non-crypto commodity, like gold, or a fiat currency, such as the US dollar. And, unlike a fiat-backed stablecoin, backed by a regular currency, an algorithmic stablecoin maintains its peg by issuing or purchasing coins through a smart contract. Terra achieves this by increasing or decreasing the availability of the LUNA token.

Aave (AAVE)

In the DeFi ecosystem, Aave is a relatively well-known player. It's a decentralized lending platform where anyone can use their crypto assets to borrow, lend, and earn interest. Users may deposit cryptocurrency they desire to invest into a lending pool. They may then take out loans from the pools, with interest on those who put their assets first. It works the same way a typical bank does with your money, but you get a bigger proportion of the loan interest because there is no intermediary.

There's always the possibility that newer DeFi cryptos will overcome older ones. However, in terms of total value locked, Aave remains at the top of DeFi Llama's list of lenders (the amount of money on the platform). It updated to Aave v2 at the end of 2020 and now runs on the Ethereum (ETH), Avalanche (AVAX), and Polygon (MATIC) networks, removing the need for users to pay Ethereum's exorbitant gas fees.

Chainlink (LINK)

We need to understand oracles and smart contracts to comprehend Chainlink. Smart contracts are bits of code that run independently when specific conditions are met. For example, a farmer would get weather insurance, and the smart contract would payout if the meteorological circumstances were to occur. Oracles gather the data that smart contracts rely on to activate; without them, the smart contract would be unable to do so. And when it comes to oracles, Chainlink is the market leader.

Several prominent DeFi solutions use chainlink's oracle data. However, this behind-the-scenes worker has so far failed to pique investor interest. LINK barely increased roughly 70% in 2021, despite various well-known analysts highlighting its potential. That's a significant rise, but not as important as some others.

Top DeFi Trends in 2022

Traditional Financial Products That Have Debut in the DeFi Ecosystem

Some estimate that the total value of financial derivatives in traditional financial markets is ten times that of global GDP. Derivatives, in essence, reduce the value of traditional financial markets. On the other hand, the DeFi derivatives market is still in its infancy. The DeFi derivatives market now has a TVL of $2.16 billion, or around 3% of the whole DeFi market. However, its recent expansion has been phenomenal. In late 2020, the DeFi derivatives market's TVL was about $875 million. In less than two years, the market has risen by around thrice.

The major participant in this market is dYdX, and it accounts for more than 40% of the whole DeFi derivatives market. Synthetix is another major participant. Synthetix has essentially built an environment where consumers may gain exposure to assets and commodities without dealing with an intermediary. Synthetix develops Synths that effectively replicate the price behavior of the asset or item they are tracking (such as gold, oil, US dollar, or Bitcoin). On Sythetix's decentralized exchange, Kwenta, you may trade Synths (along with inverse Synths). Synthetix has also developed two synthetic indices, one for DeFi assets and the other for controlled exchange tokens.

Wrapped Bitcoin (WBTC) is another example of the crypto market's successful derivatives usage to boost efficiency. WBTC is essentially a means to construct a bitcoin derivative based on Ethereum. Owners of Bitcoin may then use their derivative form of the currency to lend, stake, or yield income on the Ethereum blockchain. The supply of WBTC increased from 600 BTC to 124,000 BTC in 2020. WBTC accounted for almost 1% of the entire bitcoin supply in late 2020. According to some estimates, that amount might rise to 5% by early 2022, allowing for a wide range of cross-platform transactions.

There is even wrapped Ethereum (WETH). After the introduction of ETH, the ERC-20 token standard (which you can use in many smart contract transactions) was created. Many ETH holders wish to convert their ETH to an ERC-20 token. WETH holders can do so. It also looks to be rather popular. According to reports, over 5% of ETH was converted into WETH in September of 2020. 2020 saw the manufacturing of over 5.5 million WETH.

Traditional financial instruments such as options contracts are gaining traction in the crypto world. Hegic is the most popular platform for trading crypto-based options. The Hegic platform, in essence, allows users to participate in on-chain option contracts for ETH and WBTC. Hegic has made it simpler for crypto holders and minors to manage their risks and particular short assets. Hegic thinks that the overall ETH average daily options volume was around $50-$120 million in December 2020. And BTC's daily options volume was between $300 and $800 million. Hegic estimates that the total daily trading volume of both ETH and BTC options will reach $9.2 billion by 2023. If this scenario comes to fruition, the BTC and ETH option markets will be valued around ten times what they are currently.

Tranche financing is another type of financial innovation finding its way from traditional banking to the crypto ecosystem. In the financial industry, Tranche lending products allow lenders to fund more unpredictable and riskier loans by pooling loans and distributing the revenues to groups of investors according to risk appetite. The asset exposure is well-balanced. The owners of the tranche loan product may also determine how much risk they want to take on. Lower-risk investors receive the aggregated interest first, whereas higher-risk investors receive riskier income that may or may not be paid. Tranche lending is pioneered in the crypto realm by protocols like BarnBridge and Saffron Finance. In the crypto world, this is more vital than ever. With the tranche lending mechanism, obtaining reliable fixed income is possible despite the inherent volatility of crypto assets.

The growth of DeFi and DeFi derivative products is driving the increase in DeFi insurance. In many aspects, these insurance contracts are identical to traditional insurance. On the other hand, DeFi insurance works in a fully decentralized method, matching DeFi users wishing to earn money with those looking to decrease risk. Nexus Mutual, for example, is a DeFi insurance platform that allows ETH investors to pool their assets to ensure other smart contracts. Insurance buyers contribute a premium to this pool in exchange for a payout if the insured risk occurs. Nexus Mutual has increased its market capitalization from over $4 million TVL in July 2020 to around $250 million TVL in February 2021. In February 2022, it quadrupled in a year, reaching moreover $500 million. Bridge Mutual makes it simple for anybody to earn money by providing coverage or safeguarding their assets by purchasing coverage. Bridge Mutual, like Nexus Mutual, offers peer-to-peer insurance for stablecoins, cryptocurrency exchanges, and smart contracts. The platform raised $1.6 million in a private offering, which was $9 million oversubscribed.

Expect financial products like insurance, derivatives, and tranche or collateralized lending to become more critical as the DeFi business grows.

DeFi Seeks to Monetize Blockchain Gaming

There are about 2 billion gamers in the world. They also spend more than $159 billion every year, and that figure is estimated to be over $256 billion by 2025. With increasing individuals devoting hours to this form of entertainment, players and developers are looking for new ways to profit.

Blockchain gaming is one method that creators are attempting to monetize their work. These video games, in essence, are run on a blockchain rather than a central server. Players can "mine" tokens by completing specific game tasks. In-game transferability will need the use of well-known DeFi protocols. And many game-based cryptocurrency owners will most likely seek to make a profit on their investments.

According to a Toptal poll, 62% of gamers and 82% of developers are interested in generating and investing in digital assets that you can transfer between games. The crypto world has since caught up to their wishes. HashCraft, the first blockchain video game, was released by Ubisoft in 2019. Several names have now been released. BitSport, a cryptocurrency gaming platform, said in 2020 that it would create a means for cryptocurrency owners to fund professional players and stake competitions. BitSport stablecoin holders may essentially bet their tokens on future competitions to earn interest. They can also back a player and profit from a portion of their wins.

Cross-Chain Technology to Solve Scalability Problems

The rising transaction fees are issues linked with the DeFi ecosystem's fast expansion. The quickly rising Ethereum gas is an illustration of this. Ethereum gas is the fee paid for a transaction on the Ethereum blockchain. The supply and demand for computing power required to perform network transactions determine the gas fee.

Since 2020, the average transaction charge has risen rapidly, reaching over $69 per transaction in May of 2021. High gas fees have also been a factor in the record DeFi liquidations on February 22 and 23, 2021. The influx of new users utilizing DeFi apps on the Ethereum blockchain has made the entire network slower and growing transaction prices. Several crypto projects are beginning to offer the cross-chain capability to overcome this problem.

Essentially, cross-chain technology aims to make transactions and smart contracts possible from one chain to another. This compatibility is expected to make DeFi solutions scale far more easily than on the Ethereum network alone. Polkadot has been the most successful pioneer in this field. You can transfer tokens, data, and other assets on the Polkadot network between blockchains, and users can even develop their blockchains. It also improves transaction efficiency by distributing transactions over numerous parallel blockchains. The Polkadot governance currency (DOT) reached almost $50 in 2021, up from around $10 in August. There are now a few DeFi apps created on Polkadot's network, and the most popular is undoubtedly equilibrium.

In the year 2020, it switched to the Polkadot network. Equilibrium aims to establish a DeFi ecosystem that allows users to lend, stake, trade assets, and construct smart contracts across several blockchains. Equilibrium moved one step closer to this goal in February of 2021. Curve Finance, the world's largest crypto automated market maker (AMM), has announced that it will launch an exchange on the Polkadot network. In February 2021, Avalanche, another multi-blockchain network, announced its Avalanche-Ethereum Bridge platform. The technology is essentially a new DeFi network that will make transactions more efficient and less expensive. Pangolin, a decentralized exchange, is one of the Dapps that the project aims to attract. Cross-chain interoperability has been a success for the Poly Network.

It has partnered with Binance, the world's largest cryptocurrency exchange, to allow Dapps created on either the Binance Smart Chain or the Poly Network to run on both platforms. The Blockchain Services Network (BSC) has also employed the Poly Network to provide cross-chain interoperability. You can use the BSC, run by the Chinese government, to establish a "blockchain internet."

DeFi Use Cases in 2022

You might wonder what DeFi could be used for. DeFi use cases and examples may help you understand the whole concept of decentralized finance. Now let's look at some popular DeFi applications in 2022.

Asset Management

One of the most significant advantages of DeFi is having more control over your possessions. As a result, many of the most promising DeFi projects include services that allow users to manage their virtual assets. As a result, individuals may profit from their virtual assets. Individuals who use DeFi may protect their personal information. Previously, you had to share your bank account information or private keys with other companies.

Thanks to projects like Metamask, Argent, and Gnosis Safe, it's now possible to protect and store these pieces of data on a user's platform. As a result, only account holders will have access to and control their funds. Users may benefit from decentralized finance in various ways, including asset management.

Decentralized Autonomous Organizations (DAOs)

The use of DAOs, which are the equivalent of regulated financial organizations, is one of the pillars of DeFi. In the current structure, centralized banking companies play a significant role, and these organizations are in charge of vital financial functions such as raising cash, managing resources, and creating governance. Decentralized organizations might achieve the same goals in a Blockchain-based ecosystem. Decentralized autonomous organizations (DAOs), on the other hand, are self-contained and do not have to adhere to the limits set by central authorities.

Risk Analysis and Prevention Tools

Because of openness and decentralization, people could locate and assess unprecedented data. Users may use this data to make more creative business decisions, uncover new economic opportunities, and improve risk management strategies. As a result of this technological advancement, useable blockchain apps and platforms have created a new data analysis. For example, DeFi Pulse and CoDeFi Data are analytics and risk management solutions that add value to the table. Today, organizations are very flexible due to unanticipated economic rewards, one of the most critical decentralized financial applications.

Synthetic Resources and Derivatives

One of the more intriguing DeFi use cases has been the creation of blockchain-enabled derivatives using intelligent contracts. The value of an asset rather than the actual contract value determines the contract's value. This underlying economic asset, like traditional securities, might include a wide range of items, including but not limited to debt instruments such as bonds and fiat money, commodities, market indices, borrowing costs, and share prices.

Tokenized derivatives are now treated as additional securities and their value swings in lockstep with the underlying assets. As a result, derivatives generate whole new assets. Among the most famous DeFi attempts are blockchain-enabled derivatives ventures like Synthetix and dYdX.

Infrastructure Tools

The components of a DeFi system can be linked and interoperated.

Composability is a design feature that serves as a foundation for infrastructure development. As a result of the network effect, DeFi projects are continually merging. The development of infrastructure tools is one of the most critical applications of DeFi. Two notable DeFi projects that exemplify this are TruffleSuite and InfuraAPI.

Digital Identification

Blockchain-based digital identity systems have lately garnered a lot of traction. DeFi protocols in conjunction with many digital identification technologies may benefit users. Traditionally, a person's wages or the value of their assets determines their credit rating. Thanks to this new digital identity, you can now access DeFi apps anywhere with an internet connection.

Insurance

Insurance is a large financial business that has proven to be a vital DeFi use case. It's time to eliminate the current insurance system's clumsy documentation, old auditing methods, and inefficient administrative insurance payout processes. If we deploy smart contracts effectively, we can address many of the current system's issues. Several DeFi projects provide insurance against smart contracts or DeFi risks (Nexus Mutual, Opyn, and VouchForMe).

eSports and Gaming

Gaming has progressed a long way from its humble beginnings as a source of entertainment. New games now include in-app purchases and treasure chests, and these aspects allow gamers to spend real-world money on new cosmetics for their heroes and gadgets. You can use DeFi tokens to create various entertainment systems due to DeFi's API. People are more creative than ever, and they are more eager to try new technologies.

Margin Trading

Margin trading is a big part of traditional trading. Put another way; it's the practice of borrowing small amounts of money from intermediaries to invest and earn right away. With DeFi, entrepreneurs no longer need to rely on intermediaries for funding, and you can accomplish this by enacting a decentralized credit policy using smart contracts. DeFi startups have already implemented such lending blockchain protocols, and this activity is referred to as the independent money market.

DeFi Emerging Platforms in 2022

To help you identify some potential coins, here is a list of emerging and promising DeFi projects worth following in 2022.

Starly

Starly is a decentralized exchange platform that focuses on internal community support and low transaction fees (0.1 percent). Starly is a decentralized autonomous organization (DAO) that allows users to trade, earn, and stake Binance Smart Chain (BSC) tokens. Starly aimed to meet the demands for DeFi solutions as quickly as possible while also allowing community members to show their preferences. Because of its improved speed and reduced transaction costs, BSC allows the Starly community to get the most out of the platform. The platform's primary objective is to serve the needs of the Starly community. Starly is built on the ideas of an open DEX platform, promoting a free, open, and fair financial system based on high-quality goods and services.

Token STLY

STLY is a utility token that serves as the foundation for the Starly ecosystem, and it is a tool for engaging on the Starly platform. The token is only starting to gain attention, but it has a lot of promise. Furthermore, you will have access to various unique perks available to token holders.

The supply of tokens is reduced when they are burned. A team of developers at Starly is burning tokens based on the community's interests to raise the token's value. The current balance of burnt tokens is shown in the blockchain and is open to the public. As a result, the token's value continues to rise, benefiting the community.

Kyber Network

When trading various tokens via Kyber, the protocol compensates liquidity providers in the form of spreads. Because the DeFi ecosystem is still relatively young, substantial price volatility is expected due to limited liquidity, which allows for manipulation by large players. Kyber Network operates as a middleman between buyers and sellers to overcome this problem.

Kyber Network is a blockchain-based network that pools liquidity from various sources to assure transaction speed and security. The KNC coin has risen by 155 percent since its inception in July 2020 and is now worth $4,217 per coin. More KNC coins will be consumed over time, leading to growth if the token's demand stays strong.

Serum

Serum is a decentralized cryptocurrency exchange based on the Solana protocol. It offers fast transactions at cheap rates. It is based on the Solana blockchain and is open to everybody. It was created by the FTX exchange, which provides access to derivatives like options, volatility-based products, and cryptocurrency futures contracts. It has a cheap transaction fee of $0.00001 for each transaction and executes orders quickly. Because it draws high-frequency traders and market makers, it is one of the most promising DeFi projects.

The system leverages all commissions traders pay on the Serum network to acquire and burn SRM tokens. As a result, the supply is steadily dwindling.

Dear Reader,

As independent authors it's often difficult to gather reviews compared to much bigger publishers.

Therefore, please leave a review on the platform where you bought this book.

Many thanks,

Author Team

Want Free New Book Launches?

Email "DEFI 2022" to:

mindsetmastership@gmail.com

CHAPTER 2

HOW TO INVEST AND
EARN WITH DEFI IN 2022

DeFi is an open-source, rapidly-growing alternative to traditional financial services that requires only a crypto wallet to access many possibilities, ranging from mortgages to investments. Making a DeFi investment could involve deploying assets as liquidity on decentralized exchanges (DEXs) and lending and borrowing utilizing DeFi lending protocols; yield farming through liquidity pools to gain long-term passive income. DeFi tokens have seen dramatic growth due to wide use as a means for users to access previously unavailable technologies.

Now let's look at some new and promising ways to invest and profit from the DeFi ecosystem.

Lend and Earn

Traditional finance (TradFi) relies on a central entity such as a bank to provide services like lending and borrowing. In contrast, DeFi relies on protocols written by developers to offer similar services. Take, for example, lending. Unlike tradFi, lending in the DeFi ecosystem may yield substantially higher yearly interest rates (5% to 30%). Second, interacting with these services has been simplified because all required is a wallet. Third, the loan amount is excessively collateralized. For instance, if a user wants to borrow $1,000 in Ethereum from you (the lender), he must deposit a little more, say $1200, so that if the borrowed amount falls below the amount placed, he gets liquidated. This ensures that you (the lender) get paid for your initial investment. As a result, lenders receive their funds with less risk. Curve, Aave, and Yearn are some of the popular DeFi lending protocols.

Liquidity - A Riskier Approach

A market's ability to function depends on its ability to maintain liquidity. By bringing buyers and sellers together, financial markets produce liquidity. In tradFi, an exchange typically supplies all token liquidity through an order book, and customers who trade pay the exchange transaction fees. An order book list all buys and sell orders for a certain asset with a matching engine that aids in the execution of these transactions. The order book is replaced by automated market makers (AMMs) without human interaction in DeFi.

Any crypto asset owner may supply liquidity to these AMMs and profit from the fees paid by individuals who trade via them. The daily transaction fees (for example, 0.25 percent x daily transaction volume on SushiSwap) and pool share determine the rewards. The disadvantage is the chance of impermanence loss, which occurs every time the price of a crypto asset changes. If an investor wishes to be a liquidity provider, they should start with Uniswap, Spookyswap, and Pancakeswap.

Airdrops

Airdrops are among the most successful and well-proven methods for blockchain networks to attract a larger audience. Airdrops are crypto prizes offered to early members in an ecosystem to encourage them to utilize the network more and tell others about it. Ethereum Naming System (ENS), Uniswap (UNI), Stellar (XLM), dYdX (DYDX), and others have all received valuable airdrops in the past. Early adopters of these ecosystems were lavishly compensated ($1,000 on average in the case of ENS) simply for using their products or services. In general, blockchain explorers get rewarded in some way through Airdrops.

Hodl DeFi Tokens

If you're unfamiliar with crypto jargon, "hodl" means "to hold." Purchasing a token for a specific decentralized finance project is one of the easiest methods to invest in the DeFi ecosystem. The majority of DeFi projects and platforms have their cryptocurrency or token. You effectively purchase "shares" in the project by buying and holding these coins. The value of the tokens should rise if the project or platform is successful and grows.

Some DeFi tokens can generate considerable profits over time, depending on adoption levels. Yearn Finance, for example, increased in value to the point that it even outperformed Bitcoin in terms of returns in 2020. Yearn Finance coin is currently valued at over $31,000, and it's a promising option to consider.

DeFi Projects for Investments

Here is a list of some of the best DeFi projects to watch for in 2022.

Aave (AAVE)

Aave is a DeFi lending protocol that allows users to deposit crypto assets for APY incentives and then borrow more crypto assets against that collateral. It uses smart contracts instead of intermediaries like banks to allow users to borrow, lend, and earn interest on their crypto. And AAVE is the protocol's "native token," allowing holders to interact with it. It may also be staked, which rewards people who possess it. The Aave protocol makes it simpler to set up lending pools. You may put part of your cryptocurrency into a pool if you wish to lend it. Aave pools are open to anybody who wishes to borrow deposited assets as long as they offer acceptable security.

How it Works

The native AAVE token and aTokens are the two tokens issued by the system. AAVE tokens offer cost savings or free access to elements of the protocol's services and voting rights in the protocol's governance. Lenders who put money into lending pools are given tokens that allow them to obtain interest payments. For instance, if you deposit ETH, you will get aETH, which will be converted to ETH when you withdraw ETH from Aave.

Aave also provides flash loans to users who want to take advantage of arbitrage opportunities (when a coin is valued more on one exchange than another) and optimize their revenues in the DeFi ecosystems. These loans don't require collateral and are paid back right away. The condition is that the borrowed money, plus a 0.09 percent charge, must be repaid in one transaction; otherwise, the operation will be stopped.

Keep in mind that traditional Aave loans need the borrower to provide collateral (such as ETH). Choosing your collateral is crucial if you're borrowing coins with Aave because crypto may be volatile. If your collateral falls below a threshold, it may be liquidated (which means you won't get your money back), and you may be charged extra costs. As a result, stablecoins have become a popular collateral option. Please carefully read Aave's terms & conditions.

Algorand (ALGO)

By building on similar projects like Ethereum, Algorand attempts to increase network scalability, security, and transaction time. Developers may use Algorand to create decentralized apps that benefit from quick, low-cost transaction processing while increasing the number of users.

How it Works

Using a process known as PPoS, Algorand nodes agree on what should be included on the blockchain (or "Pure Proof of Stake"). It uses a staking mechanism to validate new transactions and produce new crypto tokens (rather than a PoW mining system like Bitcoin's). Users (or nodes) in the Algorand network can stake a portion of their ALGO in exchange for the chance to propose a new block of verified transactions at random. The winner will be given a brand new ALGO.

Remember that PPoS systems like Algorand's utilize less power than Proof of Work blockchains like Bitcoin since they don't rely on thousands of miners to solve cryptographic puzzles to win a block reward and earn transaction fees.

Bitcoin Cash (BCH)

Bitcoin was created to become a digital currency that individuals could use to perform online transactions, and it has turned into a "store of wealth" similar to digital gold. Bitcoin currency was developed to carry on the original peer-to-peer cash concept – a high-volume, low-fee network available to anybody with an internet connection.

How it Works

The original Bitcoin blockchain serves as the foundation for the Bitcoin Cash blockchain. However, there are a few key differences. One of the most notable is a 32MB maximum block size, up from 1MB in Bitcoin. Bitcoin Cash can execute transactions faster than Bitcoin, with lower fees and more transactions per second, because of the increased block size. Remember that Bitcoin Cash is accepted by PayPal and is widely available on exchanges. Keep in mind that just because it's being created to be quicker and less expensive than Bitcoin doesn't indicate that people have abandoned the original in favor of the newer version.

Cardano (ADA)

Cardano aims to be a next-generation version of the Ethereum concept. It's designed to be an elegant, long-lasting, and scalable smart contract platform that will allow you to create a wide range of decentralized banking apps, new crypto assets, games, and more. You can use the native coin of the Cardano network, ADA, to store value, transmit and receive payments, stake, and pay transaction fees.

How it Works

Cardano strives to be the greenest blockchain platform currently available. It uses a unique PoS consensus process called Ouroboros instead of the energy-intensive proof-of-work approach used by Bitcoin and Ethereum. We have two levels in the Cardano blockchain: the Cardano Settlement Layer (CSL) and the Cardano Computing Layer (CCL) (CCL). The CSL is where Cardano keeps the ledger of accounts and balances (where the Ouroboros consensus mechanism validates the transactions). The CCL layer handles all calculations for blockchain-based applications that use smart contract operations.

The Cardano network can process up to a million transactions per second by splitting the blockchain into two levels. Cardano's developer team also hopes to add smart contract functionality this year.

Chainlink (LINK)

Chainlink, a decentralized oracle network, is powered by LINK Ethereum token. Oracles are a critical component of the DeFi space. In the absence of a governance system, they're the fundamental means DeFi apps obtain reliable external data (especially prices). There was no reliable mechanism for smart contracts and DeFi applications to receive external market pricing until the introduction of Chainlink.

How it Works

Chainlink was created to reward a worldwide network of computers (or "nodes") for providing reliable data to Chainlink's oracles. Today, various oracles exist, including pricing data for multiple assets, weather data, and location data. It uses the LINK token to pay for network services and motivate nodes to produce verifiably honest work and correct data. To become a node and begin giving data to Chainlink oracles, users have to stake LINK tokens in a smart contract to prevent errors or fake data on the network.

Compound (COMP)

Compound is a decentralized lending system that lets users deposit crypto assets in exchange for APY rewards and then borrow extra crypto assets with that collateral. It's one of many DeFi applications based on the Ethereum blockchain. Its native coin is COMP.

How it Works

When you give Compound an asset, you instantly start earning interest on that deposit. You can use the value of the collateral you've provided to set a borrowing limit. You get a unique cToken when you deposit Compound. For example, when you put USD Coin into Compound, you'll find cUSDC in the wallet, and as you withdraw the USDC, the cUSDC will vanish. (cUSDC may be kept, transferred, and traded the same way as any other token can.)

There is now interest in cTokens and rewards in native COMP tokens for the crypto you invest into Compound. The interest rate in any compound market is dynamic and exclusively controlled by supply and demand. Holders of COMP coins may also vote on the system's future, making Compound truly decentralized. Keep in mind that in traditional finance, "over-collateralized lending" refers to the practice of giving one asset in exchange for a loan on another. It can let investors diversify their portfolios and use complex trading tactics such as borrowing cryptocurrency to invest in other assets (but note that there are risks associated with collateralized lending, including losing your collateral).

Cosmos (ATOM)

Cosmos seeks to be the "internet of blockchains" by allowing developers to create their blockchains connected through the Cosmos network. You can use ATOM's native coin to stake and secure the "Global Hub," which combines these blockchains.

How it Works

Cosmos' major purpose is to enable decentralized programs ——

everything from NFT markets to decentralized exchanges — to run on their dedicated blockchains, making them faster and cheaper. The IBC protocol, or Inter-Blockchain Communication protocol, unites these disparate blockchains. Developers may also quickly build customized blockchains using Cosmos' prebuilt modules for particular use cases.

The Cosmos consensus engine, IBC protocol, and software development kit are designed to make it easy to use and interoperate between chains while maintaining the security, transaction cost, and speed that developers expect from other leading blockchain platforms. Remember that staking ATOM on Coinbase may result in rewards.

Dogecoin (DOGE)

For most of its history, Dogecoin (pronounced "dohj coin") was regarded as a humorous "meme coin" that was famous among its users but had little value. That changed in 2021, when it became one of the most valuable cryptocurrencies by market capitalization, with a TVL of more than $50 billion, even though each coin is only worth a few cents. The developer team created Dogecoin as a fun, low-stakes Bitcoin alternative; therefore, abundance is essential. It attracted a passionate online community almost immediately after its inception in late 2013 when it was notably used to send the Jamaican bobsled squad to the 2014 Winter Olympics in Sochi.

However, note that, unlike Bitcoin, created to be abundant and resistant to inflation, Dogecoin was created to be rare and immune to inflation. Currently, there is about 130 billion DOGE in circulation, with miners producing 10,000 every minute.

Litecoin (LTC)

One of the earliest cryptos is Litecoin. It was founded in 2011 as a fork of Bitcoin, and it offers quicker transaction speeds and reduced transaction costs.

How it Works

Litecoin did not attempt to modify the underlying logic or architecture as a fork of Bitcoin. It is basically identical to Bitcoin in terms of usage and design – but with a faster transaction time and lower transaction fee.

However, while Litecoin's speed and friendly fees make it tempting as a payment option and a method of moving value, the network has much fewer miners than Bitcoin, posing a threat to overall network security.

Solana (SOL)

Solana is one among many emerging cryptos vying for Ethereum's attention. Solana, like Ethereum, is both a cryptocurrency and a versatile platform for launching cryptocurrency projects, ranging from decentralized exchanges like Serum to NFT projects like Degenerate Apes (or DEX). Its main novelty is its quickness. Solana can perform about 50,000 transactions per second, but Ethereum can only handle 15 or less. (The ETH2 update, which is presently under progress, aims to make Ethereum substantially quicker than it currently is.)

SOL is Solana's native token. You can use SOL for staking and paying transaction fees. It also serves as a "native token," allowing users to vote on future upgrades and governance ideas proposed by the Solana community. SOL may be bought and sold on exchanges like Coinbase.

How it Works

Solana provides fast transaction speeds by combining the proof-of-stake consensus mechanism with a unique "proof of history" methodology. Proof of history is a way of keeping time on a decentralized network without requiring all computers to communicate and agree on it. Like Ethereum, Solana is a computer platform that can interact with smart contracts. Smart contracts are used in various applications, from NFT markets and DeFi to games and decentralized lotteries. Because speeds are quick and minimal congestion, users may choose a Solana-based service over Ethereum. This results in incredibly low prices. (However, keep in mind that new crypto applications and technology come with risks, ranging from volatility to the possibility of exploiting unforeseen smart-contract flaws.)

Buy and Hold Ethereum

If you're unsure which DeFi coins to invest in, buying and holding Ethereum or Binance smart chain tokens is safer. We use Ethereum smart contracts in several DeFi projects. Without engaging in individual DeFi projects, you may gain exposure to the DeFi industry and its potential for development by investing in Ethereum as a whole. Individual DeFi projects might require a lot of time and effort to research. There is also a greater risk because most DeFi tokens are new and have a smaller market cap than a more established cryptocurrency like Ethereum.

DeFi Index Fund

Jack Bogle created the index fund in 1975 as a mechanism for regular investors to compete with professional investors to keep up with the market rather than outperform it. Index funds have gained such a high level of confidence — and have done so well — that they now account for about half of the $9 trillion in total assets invested in equities.

How to Buy Index Fund

The method of purchasing one of the index tokens is pretty simple, thanks to Trustwallet. In the browser bar, input "indexed.finance" into the Trustwallet DApp Browser. The main page will appear prominently with the two flagship indices, DeFi5 and CC10.

CC10 covers the larger Cryptocurrency market and also includes $YFI, $MKR, $UMA, $LINK, and $OMG. DeFi5 is an index that includes five of the so-called "DeFi blue chips": $AAVE, $UNI, $SNX, $CRV, and $COMP. DeFi5 is the most popular, with $38 million AUM compared to $30 million for CC10. DeFi5 has also outpaced CC10 in the last month owing to the increasing success of UNI, AAVE, and others. However, due to other projects gradually catching up, CC10 may outperform DeFi5 in the nearest future. Follow these simple steps to invest in the index.

- Choose the index you wish to invest in.
- Click "Trade"
- Enter the amount of ETH you wish to spend.
- Press the "Swap" button
- Trust Wallet will show the transaction cost.
- Press "Send"
- And your transaction is completed

How to Stake an Index

Now that you possess an index token, you may participate in the indexed's liquidity mining scheme. Index holders who stake their index tokens or offer liquidity on Uniswap get a quarter of the $NDX token supply.

There are four pools in total:

- DEFI5 (simple staking)
- CC10 (simple staking)
- DEFI5-ETH on Uniswap
- CC10-ETH on Uniswap

Each pool will get 625,000 NDX during Phase 1 of the liquidity mining, which runs through March. You'll probably get a few less $NDX tokens when you stake your index because this option is more popular and less risky. You can also supply liquidity on Uniswap and stake your LP tokens, but this comes with risks, including impermanent loss. Follow these steps to stake an index.

- Select "stake" from the burger menu at the top.

- Choose the pool you wish to stake on.
- Select how much you want to stake
- Approve indexed to move your index tokens
- Wait for the blockchain transaction to be confirmed
- Deposit your index token

You may sit back and watch your NDX token holdings develop once you've done all of these stages. You will earn NDX tokens for staking your index tokens. You have the freedom to unstake your index token or receive your NDX award at any time. However, to save money on gas, it's usually best to claim the NDX tokens only once you've earned enough money to make it profitable.

DeFi Staking

In its most basic meaning, DeFi staking is locking crypto assets into a smart contract in return for becoming a validator in a DeFi protocol or a Layer 1 blockchain and collecting rewards for executing the tasks required of the job. We use DeFi staking to refer to all DeFi actions that entail a temporary commitment of crypto assets.

Types of DeFi Staking

Staking

The simplest form of staking is securing a certain quantity of crypto assets to become a validator in a PoS blockchain network. Unlike Proof of Labor consensus techniques, which require a lot of energy-intensive computing work to ensure transaction validity, PoS depends on validators who have a stake in the network's success through their staked crypto assets. In other words, validators must carry out their responsibilities meticulously or risk losing a portion or possibly all of their stakes. Validators can now get staking incentives for producing and validating blocks, which incentivizes good conduct even more.

Ethereum is now the most well-known Proof of Stake blockchain, as part of the Eth2 (Ethereum 2.0) project, migrating from Proof of Work to Proof of Stake. Polkadot and The Graph are two more noteworthy examples.

At its most basic level, the staking procedure is an interested party posting a 'bond' (stake) to become a network validator, making that person eligible for staking rewards. The difficulty with this straightforward staking method is that the stakes are usually rather large. To become a validator on Eth2's Beacon Chain, you must deposit 32 ETH, a significant sum. As a result, most ordinary investors are priced out of staking chances.

Fortunately, staking service providers have emerged, allowing customers to avoid the prohibitive cost requirements. Then there are the so-called staking pools, which would enable users to pool their staking cash with other crypto investors. People can deposit any quantity of tokens into a staking pool and begin receiving passive income based on the percentage of the pool's total holdings that their contribution accounts for. Users can also resort to a crypto exchange for DeFi staking services, as most large controlled and decentralized exchanges do.

Yield Farming

While lending and borrowing platforms were the first major use of decentralized finance, yield farming demonstrated DeFi's ultimate potential. The word refers to the practice of shifting crypto assets across several DeFi staking sites. People essentially make their assets available to a lending protocol or liquidity pool in exchange for passive income as interest and a part of the revenue earned by their preferred platform. However, they may quickly transfer their money to different pools and platforms to pursue higher-yielding investments.

Investing in various assets to maximize your earning potential or hedging against unanticipated risks is one of the most common investing methods in traditional financial markets. On the other hand, DeFi staking allows investors to switch between several DeFi protocols with little to no downtime because of the combination of 24/7 access to markets, smart-contract-driven automation, and the lack of intermediaries. You can develop DeFi staking strategies in many ways with such a wide range of options. We will discuss in-depth yield farming later in the book.

Liquidity Mining

Liquidity mining is yield farming in which crypto assets are provided to liquidity pools. These pools are critical for facilitating trading on Auto Market Maker (AMM) decentralized crypto exchanges (DEXs) without the need for intermediaries. A primary liquidity pool comprises the two assets that make up a trading pair – for example, ETH/DAI – and uses an algorithm to ensure that one of the assets' values is always equal to the other. This implies that the pool adjusts the prices of the assets in real-time to account for any changes in their respective values due to trading. In our ETH/DAI example, buying ETH reduces the quantity of ETH in the pool while raising the amount of DAI.

Liquidity providers, who make their assets accessible to liquidity pools, are at the system's heart. Liquidity providers get compensated in many ways, including a share of the fees received by the pool. Some DeFi staking systems provide their tokens as part of their rewards.

Best DeFi Coins to Buy for 2022 and Beyond

To select the best DeFi coins for your investment portfolio, you'll need to evaluate the following metrics:

- Current market capitalization
- Potential for growth
- Past performance
- Goals and milestones on the journey map
- The cost of a token
- Exchanges that have the token listed

Considering these key factors, here is a list of the best DeFi coins for 2022 with growth potential.

Lucky Block – Overall Best DeFi Coin to Buy in 2022

Lucky Block emerged as the apparent winner among DeFi coins and the most acceptable DeFi coin to invest in. The project, which started in late 2021, is nearing the completion of the introduction of an innovative lottery game platform. To summarize, the Lucky Block lottery ecosystem differs from traditional operators in that all gaming outcomes are decentralized.

Uniswap - The Best DEX and The Most Popular DeFi Coin

Uniswap is a novel exchange platform that allows traders to swap tokens peer-to-peer. This project exemplifies the concept of decentralized finance. To put it another way, Uniswap eliminates the need for a centralized intermediary when buying and selling crypto assets.

Terra – The Leading DeFi Coin That Keeps Outperforming the Market

There's no doubt that the global cryptocurrency markets, particularly those for DeFi coins, have been overwhelmingly pessimistic heading into 2022. With that considered, the value of Terra – which continues to perform exceptionally well – looks to be unstoppable. Terra is a decentralized financial initiative that specializes in algorithmic stablecoins for those who are unfamiliar.

Decentraland – Invest in the Metaverse via the MANA Token

The Metaverse will grow in popularity in the future, with companies like Facebook renaming their firm Meta Platforms. Consequently, if you want to get in on the ground floor of this developing concept, you may buy MANA tokens, Decentraland's original digital asset. Decentraland is a project built on the Ethereum blockchain that provides everyone access to a virtual game environment. Users may buy virtual land and then create digital real estate on Decentraland, one of the platform's most unique aspects.

Yearn.finance – DeFi Services Through Decentralized Lending Agreements

This project specializes in decentralized financial services, emphasizing peer-to-peer loans at writing. Yearn.finance acts as a conduit between borrowers and lenders, eliminating the need for a centralized middleman. This is made possible through smart contract technology, which allows people to utilize Yearn.finance to borrow money without a credit check. Investors that wish to earn a return on their idle bitcoin assets support these loans.

AAVE – Open Source DeFi Protocol

AAVE deems itself an open-source liquidity protocol that connects peer-to-peer lenders and investors. Investors may inject crypto tokens into lending pools in exchange for interest using the AAVE platform. The APY given will be determined by the Token in question. However, the money is disbursed to borrowers, who must supply a security deposit to get immediate cash. The AAVE token is presently the most valuable DeFi currency in market capitalization and value. You would have spent only $53 for the Token when it debuted in 2020, and AAVE was trading for over $262 by 2022, a gain of about 400 percent.

Top DeFi Investment Tips

So, there are a few pointers on making a DeFi investment.

Take a Peek at The Sky

Looking for DeFi platforms and projects that can lead their respective categories is an intelligent approach to start your DeFi investment career. Whether these DeFi projects are now leaders in their sectors or can create a new one, they exist in the DeFi space is enough to make them star enterprises if they become leaders. You may be familiar with the term "star venture," which refers to a company that is the market leader in a high-growth category. Star projects can frequently dominate their niches for long periods due to network effects, greater cash flow and access to resources, momentum, and an X-Factor.

You may detect a star by looking for individuals who are carving out a new niche in DeFi or those who are dominating theirs. To illustrate this concept, let's look at a case study from DeFi's Paleolithic age: 2020.

Liquidity mining is causing a stir at the DeFi TVL. Let's look at how this has played out in practice over the previous few years. The years 2019 and 2020, and 2021 were highly influential in DeFi's history. First, Compound Finance's groundbreaking idea of liquidity mining launched what we now refer to as the "DeFi Summer of 2020." Between April and September 2020, DeFi had unprecedented growth and development, with the industry's TVL increasing from $800 million to $10 billion. Compound's investors, meanwhile, performed handsomely throughout the process.

DeFi had another great year in 2021. However, in 2021, several new sub-niches arose, with emerging blockchains eager to join the trend. In 2021, Ethereum was no longer the only choice for people interested in DeFi. Despite losing market share, Ethereum-based DeFi expanded by more than 6-fold over the year. This exemplifies the star principle at work and, perhaps paradoxically, lays the groundwork for a different way to invest in DeFi.

Explore New Ecosystems

The percentage of TVL in DeFi per blockchain reveals a clear trend: Ethereum is losing market share, owing to its high gas prices, which prevent individuals without large sums of money from participating. After Ethereum's proof-of-stake emerges, it'll be fascinating to observe if the territory Ethereum has lost to other blockchains continues to trend in the same manner. Meanwhile, quicker blockchains like Terra and Binance Smart Chain have had a chance to contend for a significant second position. Solana and Avalanche have also taken advantage of this by absorbing market value.

This throws up fascinating opportunities for investors since it appears that, with TVL on the table, investing in new DeFi ecosystems might be a good option. The star system remains true if we consider each new blockchain's niche. Yes, the world's leading DeFi 2.0 liquidity platform would be a star in and of itself, but so would the world's leading Fantom 2.0 liquidity solution. In this way, your DeFi investment can be chain agnostic.

Be aware of distinctions between the number of protocols and the TVL while studying how to invest in DeFi. Existing evidence shows that TVL does not scale linearly with the number of protocols in an ecosystem. While BSC has more than half of the protocols in Ethereum, its market share is around 10%. The number of protocols is still helpful to measure how broad and well-rounded an ecosystem is since it indicates how many different options are available.

DeFi is also composable, implying that various protocols can combine as underlying mechanisms that others can use. In short, numbers are helpful, but they don't reveal the whole picture. When investing in a new DeFi platform, it's important to remember that some protocols are more likely to accumulate TVL. When it comes to categorizing DeFi dApps, lending and decentralized exchanges seem to get the most attention. This comes as no surprise, given that they were the first DeFi applications to appear on the Ethereum blockchain.

Consider using a data-driven strategy. When deciding how to invest in DeFi, a user can consider several aspects. Data is everywhere, although it contradicts itself at times and, to be honest, may be somewhat perplexing at times; however, data show that you're in the right direction if you can locate a project that satisfies the five criteria listed below.

- **The consistent growth of TVL**

TVL indicates how confident investors entrust their funds to a project. Exploits, rug pulls, and flaws in smart contracts are all too common in DeFi. Therefore, investors should constantly be on the lookout and take security audits seriously. A continuous increase in TVL is a good indicator for this reason. It's worth noting that we say steady rather than quick. Continuous TVL collection is preferred over fast, strong spikes, resulting in more extensive dives over time.

As an investor, it's easy to get FOMO into buying projects with a 50%+ TVL gain in a week. This, on the other hand, is not a winning approach. In all circumstances, a steady lineup indicates that a project has earned its TVL without causing any problems for investors. When it comes to TVL, it's also a good idea to compare its growth to Bitcoin or Ethereum. In this manner, you can discover that a rumored killing spree in which TVL rose by several percentage points was just the product of the two most popular cryptocurrencies pushing the market higher.

- **Middle-of-the-pack TVL**

Any blockchain project can fall into one of the following categories when assessing its investment potential:

1. A DeFi project with uncertain development potential (TVL worth substantially more than $20 million).
2. Too new and risky ($15 million in TVL and under).
3. Projects with a lot of room for expansion (about $20 million in TVL).

This metric isn't perfect (no data point is), but projects in the first group have generally accomplished what they set out to do. This suggests that, while they can be stars, they aren't at the peak of their development. They may expand with the crypto/DeFi market (which isn't terrible) or decrease if better, more project rivals emerge. You'll note that this touches on each investor's risk appetite. Some people will try to hit home runs, while others will ride the DeFi wave, which still has a long way.

The second group now includes a few projects with insufficient information to assess if they have a decent chance of becoming market leaders. On the other hand, these projects are appropriate for institutional investors or venture capital firms with unique insights and helpful information. However, research suggests that these investments may be risky for the average retail investor.

- **A high MC/FDV ratio**

FDV, or fully-diluted valuation (FDV), represents the potential market cap (MC) considering the current price and the token's maximum supply. All the tokens have been mined, produced, and issued, and the MC/FDV ratio measures how many tokens are on the market. When this ratio is too low, the steady influx of new tokens will undoubtedly outperform the protocol's growth, and the price of the protocol will most likely plummet from the present levels. Further supply increase is unlikely to substantially influence the token's cost, closely matching the protocol's TVL growth when it reaches 1. A low-but-reasonable MC/FDV ratio is at least 0.05 (or 5%) for projects with excellent development potential and more for previously established ones.

- **A lower MC/TVL ratio**

We've previously demonstrated the value of TVL as a symbol of investor confidence in a protocol. As a result, since the market cap represents the value investors place on a project, it makes sense to track the TVL closely. Token holders are almost always involved in the governance of DeFi projects. As a result, they buy tokens that determine what happens to locked money at a price too close to (or even more significant than) the TVL makes no sense.

This statistic might be the most accurate way to assess a DeFi protocol's price. An MC/TVL ratio equal to or more than 1.0 indicates that the project is either somewhat or overpriced, implying that the token price can only go down. A ratio less than 0.5, on the other hand, should mean excellent news and might indicate a wave of growth that hasn't yet been priced in.

- **Price stability of tokens**

You could be drawn to gleaming 20 percent+ rallies. Even then, abrupt price increases like this are usually signs of unhealthy market responses and malevolent pumps, particularly in low/medium market cap tokens that are more prone to price manipulation. In contrast, cryptocurrencies have democratized access to financial instruments. Most internet content is generated or intended for novice investors, a negative element in the DeFi sector. This type of investor works in a brief period, making them more prone to making mistakes.

Many DeFi investors examine a token's short-term performance before purchasing it and then hunt for reasons to justify their rash purchase. Aside from looking at performance versus BTC and ETH, the standard deviation is a good metric of price stability when looking at price changes. A lower figure indicates continuous growth/decline, which is more reliable than high but unsteady increases.

A Short message from the Author:

Hey, are you enjoying the book? I'd love to hear your thoughts!

Many readers do not know how hard reviews are to come by, and how much they help an author.

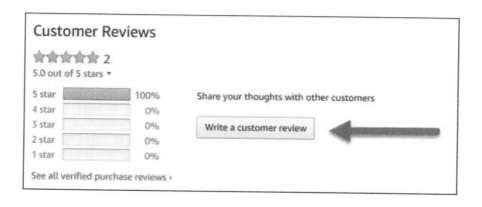

I would be incredibly thankful if you could take just 60 seconds to write a brief review on Amazon, even if it's just a few sentences!

>> Click HERE to leave a brief review on Amazon.

Thank you for taking the time to share your thoughts!

Your review will genuinely make a difference for me and help gain exposure for my work.

CHAPTER 3

DEFI YIELD FARMING IN 2022

Basics of Yield Farming

Yield farming is a way of profiting from Bitcoin ownership. DeFi yield farming is staking or lending crypto assets inside DeFi protocols to generate significant returns in interest, incentives, or extra cryptocurrency. The word "farming" means high-interest levels derived from the liquidity of various DeFi protocols. DeFi protocols also create tokens that reflect a user's portion of the liquidity pool, which may be moved to other platforms to increase their possible earnings.

Lenders and borrowers benefit from yield farming. Borrowers searching for margin trading may benefit from a liquidity pool, while lenders can create passive income by investing idle crypto assets in their wallets. In a DeFi ecosystem, yield farmers act as banks, lending money to anyone who wants to use their tokens to make more money. Smart contracts built on the blockchain, which connect borrowers and lenders while managing investment incentives, power the whole ecosystem.

Types of Yield Farming

With liquidity pool or LP farms and staking farms, you may find two different types of yield farming. The difference between the two is seen in the underlying smart contract. Better awareness of the many forms of yield production or farming methods might aid in a more thorough understanding of yield farming.

Liquidity Pool or LP Farms

Users must deposit crypto assets in a smart contract configured to supply a liquidity pool in this system. The operation of such collections is similar to that of a decentralized trading pair comprising two or more cryptocurrencies. Only the cryptocurrencies provided by the liquidity providers are available for trading in the LP farms. Liquidity providers get rewarded with LP tokens in exchange for deposits in DeFi applications. The yield farming token might aid in retrieving deposits underpinning the liquidity pool at any moment and the increased interest in trading fees.

Liquidity provider tokens are necessary because DeFi applications that run liquidity mining algorithms create staking interfaces for depositing the tokens. Consequently, you'll be able to lock in your liquidity and get rewarded with automatic and ongoing governance token payouts.

Stake Farms

Stake farming is another method of increasing yields that have attracted the interest of investors. The process entails a user investing crypto assets into a smart contract configured to provide a staking pool. However, the staking pool is not the same as a decentralized trading pair; instead, it functions as a decentralized vault for a particular asset. The stake farming method of yield farming does not allow for trade and instead concentrates on securing deposits. Compared to liquidity pool farms, stake farms may provide a more simplified experience for users. Also, unlike operating as a liquidity provider on a decentralized exchange, stake farms only require users to deposit a single asset to generate passive revenue. They then concentrate on staking the liquidity provider tokens.

Other Yield Farming Variants

You don't have to limit yourself to liquidity pool and stake farming if you want to learn more about yield farming in crypto. Many new DeFi projects have launched new liquidity mining schemes, with new types of DeFi activities linked to governance tokens as incentives. Here are some of the various kinds of yield farming that may help you fully comprehend how DeFi yield farming works.

Insurance Mining

Insurance mining is solely focused on yield farms to compensate customers who must deposit assets in decentralized insurance funds. Successful insurance claims would be taken from the decentralized insurance funds, making them extremely hazardous. Depositors in this form of yield farming might benefit from yield farming rates on the money they put up for project protection. In the Liquity stability pool, you can clearly illustrate such a system. The LUSD stablecoin is added to the pool as a background for Liquity's lending system. Users in LQTY tokens, Liquity's native token, get the yield farming benefits.

Arbitrage Mining

Arbitrage mining is another growing example of how DeFi yield farming works from a different standpoint. Arbitrage mining is a method that focuses on yield farms that give incentives to arbitrage traders, and arbitrage traders take advantage of market inconsistencies all around the DeFi ecosystem.

Trade Mining

You might also consider trade mining to understand better how DeFi yield farming works, and it's essentially the same as arbitrage mining. However, the significant difference in this scenario immediately refers to straightforward exchanges for token payouts. Integral would be a clear illustration of an early player in trade mining. It's a decentralized exchange with a hybrid AMM/order book that has the potential to revolutionize yield farming. The network has issued ITGR, Integral governance tokens, to traders who have used the incentivized pools since its inception in March 2021.

Yield Farming Mechanism

Without talking about its mechanism, debates on yield farming rates and the process would be incomplete. The method of generating yield begins with the addition of money to liquidity pools, which are essentially smart contracts that contain funds. Liquidity pools power a marketplace where users may trade, borrow, and lend tokens. You can assume the identity of a liquidity provider after adding your cash to the liquidity pool. Users get rewarded with fees derived from the underlying DeFi platforms for the assets they have locked up.

It's vital to remember that investing in ETH isn't the same as yield farming, although lending ETH through a decentralized, non-custodial money market protocol counts as yield farming. People might deposit reward tokens in liquidity pools and move funds between different protocols to chase more significant payouts.

Yield farming is a complicated concept, and farmers must be familiar with the Ethereum network and its accompanying functions. They might then shift their cash across multiple DeFi protocols to get the highest profits. Yield farming is a problematic concept in crypto, and those who provide liquidity are rewarded based on their quantity of liquidity. As a result, farmers with large sums of money behind their capacity to provide liquidity are more likely to benefit.

Calculating Yield Farming

When it comes to determining liquidity provider returns, the following metrics are critical.

Total Value Locked (TVL)

TVL is a parametric variable that indicates how much crypto is locked up in DeFi lending and other marketplaces. You can track the TVL of cryptocurrencies in smart contracts across several platforms to provide a complete picture of their performance. It allows players to compare different DeFi systems and protocols in market share. TVL is a helpful tool for gathering liquidity in liquidity pools and a measured approach to the volume of the DeFi and yield farming markets as a whole.

Annual Percentage Yield (APY)

This is the yearly rate of return levied on borrowers and paid to suppliers.

Annual Percentage Rate (APR)

The yearly rate of return is imposed on capital borrowers but paid to capital suppliers.

You can calculate DeFi Yield farming returns every year. APR and APY are two essential variables to consider when evaluating yield farming returns. In terms of compounding impact, APR and APY are not the same. Compounding is the practice of reinvesting gains to maximize returns, and the compounding effect is considered in APY but not in APR.

Because APR and APY are traditional market measurements, DeFi must develop its own to assess yield farming returns. Simple staking processes can give up to 10% yearly returns, whereas yield farmers can use intricate trading tactics to generate over 50% annual profits.

Platforms and Protocols for Yield Farming

In the DeFi ecosystem, there are several yield farming platforms and protocols. Each platform has its own set of restrictions, risks, and yield farming strategies. The following are some of the most popular DeFi yield farming platforms.

Compound Finance

It is among the most popular platforms in the yield farming ecosystem. It is a well-known DeFi-based protocol for lending and borrowing assets. Anyone with an Ethereum wallet can contribute assets to the compound liquidity pools and earn rewards.

Yearn.Finance

The platform converts cash into yTokens. (yTokens are liquidity tokens offered to investors in return for deposits made on the Yearn.Finance platform.) It also aids in periodic rebalancing to maximize profits. This platform assists users in automatically selecting the most acceptable strategies, and its primary goal is to locate the most lucrative lending services to improve token lending.

Uniswap

Due to its frictionless nature, it is a DeFi-based DEX platform that allows users to trade tokens. These secure and straightforward token swaps help farmers in carrying out their plans. Liquidity providers deposit two tokens with equal value for market development on this platform. Traders execute deals in this liquidity pool, while liquidity providers get compensated for trades executed in the pool.

Aave

It's an open-source, non-custodial, and extensively used decentralized loan platform for yield farmers, with interest rates fluctuating dynamically according to market conditions. Lenders receive tokens in exchange for their cash after depositing the funds. These tokens are essential for permitting instant revenues and compounding interest on the amount invested. Other sophisticated features, such as flash loans, are also available.

Balancer

It's a multi-token AMM technology that lets you allocate unique tokens to the liquidity pool. Liquidity providers can use this protocol to create and configure balancer pools and profit from trade execution. Yield farmers commonly employ balancer techniques to maximize their labor due to the flexibility of creating a liquidity pool. It's identical to the Uniswap and curve protocols, except it allows you to customize token allocations in the liquidity pool.

Curve Finance

It's a decentralized exchange protocol based on Ethereum that carries out high-value exchanges using stablecoins with little slippage. It also supports the DAI, USDC, TUSD, and BTC pairings, allowing users to trade between them quickly and easily.

MakerDAO

It's one of the first DeFi projects that include a decentralized lending infrastructure to promote the development of DAI, a stablecoin tied to the US dollar. The platform is built on the Ethereum blockchain and manages crypto loans using Ethereum smart contracts. Users may store collateral assets like USDC, ETH, WBTC, or BAT in a Maker Vault and create DAI against the collateral. This loan accrues interest over time, referred to as the stability charge, which MKR token holders decide.

Synthetix

Synthetix, a synthetic protocol, issues synthetic assets on the Ethereum network. It provides a transparent price feed for various synthetic products, including gold, silver, synthetic crypto, and synthetic fiat currencies.

2022 DeFi Yield Farming Strategies

Max Risk

Most yield farming platforms contain a native token that serves as a means of interoperability. You can use the token to distribute cash as incentives, administer governance, and implement various incentive systems to keep the platform moving in the right direction.

When it comes to the tokenomics driving these incentive schemes, it's divided into two categories: tokens with an infinite supply and tokens with a fixed supply. The issue with unlimited supply tokens is that they need to retain a burn mechanism to keep the price stable. Platforms have devised many creative methods for raising revenue to burn their native token. The never-ending race to burn tokens is less of a concern; they need to find a use case for their native token to generate enough purchase pressure to offset the ongoing dumping for profit.

Why would you keep prizes that can trade for money? In DeFi, there are far too many creative ways to respond to this question. Buying the native token and staking it for rewards might be a beneficial and risky strategy that gives you the most exposure to the project's success while avoiding losing money.

Slightly Less Risk

LP Token = Platform Native Token + Network Native Token

When you deposit into the liquidity pool (LP), an LP token is created to reflect the depositor's portion in the pool as a whole. If you redeemed these LP tokens, you would receive the same assets you placed, although the actual quantities may change due to factors like a temporary loss. The majority of liquidity pools are dual asset pools, including two separate assets/tokens. The underlying assets represented by the LP token are usually shared 50/50 in most LPs. When the price of one of the underlying assets/tokens changes, the LP token rebalances itself to maintain a 50/50 ratio between the assets' values.

If you hold 1 EUR and 1 USD in an LP, if the price of USD declines, the pool will sell more EUR to acquire more USD, ensuring that the value of all assets remains 50/50. The difference in value between assets is the source of transitory loss.

So, how do we go about using the LP token? We use a decentralized exchange to deposit our LP tokens, representing our asset's liquidity pool share. The exchange will execute the trade with your assets and equitably distribute the profits. In some circumstances, if the temporary loss is too large, you could be better off keeping your two assets/tokens rather than putting them into a liquidity pool.

Medium Risk

LP Token = Volatile Token + Stable coin

Stablecoin farming is the safest strategy to guarantee your success on the yield farming platform. Stablecoins become an essential liquidity pool on any platform since most platforms require some representation of the US dollar to allow traders to unwind their speculative stakes. Combining a volatile asset/token with a stable one is safer since the asset's risk is cut by half.

Creating a volatile token + a stable coin combo is an impermanent loss waiting to happen since stablecoins are tethered to a set value. If the value of the volatile token rises, the LP will sell more of it to maintain a 50/50 value ratio between the two underlying assets in the LP. You'd have less of the volatile token and more stablecoin in the end. This method is ideal for accumulating $USD on a cryptocurrency whose value you predict will rise.

Low Risk

LP Token = Stable Token + Stable Token

Although the rates on stablecoin + stablecoin LP tokens may not appear as appealing as some of the abovementioned strategies, they significantly improve the rates offered in a typical financial context. Single asset and dual asset stable coin pools are prevalent. Because both assets are essentially the same, even while their stabilizing processes are different, there is minimal impermanent loss with dual-asset stable currency LP tokens in most circumstances. This suggests you're not overly concerned about price fluctuations.

Here are extra suggestions to help you make better Yield Farming decisions:

- A high annual percentage yield (APY) does not always imply a high rate of return

The first thing that attracts consumers is a high annual percentage yield (APY), and many projects have an initial annual percentage yield (APY) of more than 10,000 percent. It appears to be a quick method to increase your wealth. However, get answers to the following two questions:

Will the High Yield be able to last? Take a look at the high-yield timeframe. The supply could be hyper-inflated in the early days, resulting in high yields. However, within a short period, this can substantially decrease.

Will you be able to make a profit when you sell? Even if you make a significant amount during the early hyperinflation phase, you will often be unable to sell the token since the bulk of them get frozen. Check how many tokens you've earned and how many you'll be able to sell.

For example, in Luaswap, 75% of Token is frozen for the first 16 months.

- Invest in Tokens with Real-World Applications

Consider why you need the token provided by the project. For many enterprises, governance is greatly exaggerated. Is there any other use for the token except governance? Are you aware that you can UNI as collateral for loans on other platforms? That is a handy feature, and this results in UNI value. Many other DeFi coins are only money grabs with no real benefit, and they are doomed to fail.

- Invest only in Audited Projects

Ensure a reputable body audited the project and its code. When Andre Cronje revealed that he is associated with the "in production" project Eminence, people began to deposit money into his account based on his good name. On the other hand, Eminence was still a work in progress and had not been audited, and a hacker inevitably stole $15 million from the project. Quantstamp, Trail of Bits, and others are well-known auditors.

- Factor in Gas Fees in Your Profit Calculations

Remember that your actual investment is higher with today's high gas fees. Fees for (Buying Token Pairs in Uniswap + Approving Liquidity Pool Pairs in Uniswap + Approving LP Staking in the Yield Farming Protocol + Actual Staking in Yield Farming Protocol + Unstake in Yield Farming Protocol + Sell Yield Token in Uniswap + Removing Liquidity in Uniswap); it's important not to overlook this total fee. Also, include this in your profit calculation at all times.

- When do you plan to start working on the Yield Farming project?

If you enter a project late, which might be as early as the next day, you should be aware that there is already a selling push in place. This is from the first day's profit. After the first few days, the market tends to decrease. Decide whether or not you wish to enter at this time.

DeFi Yield Farming Tools

When you're yield farming, it's vital to keep track of your asset to make accurate decisions. Fortunately, several tools are available for this purpose, so make use of them.

DeFi Yield Aggregator

DeFi Prime

It's challenging to keep up with DeFi's fast-paced, ever-changing environment, and this is where DeFi Prime enters the picture. The platform neatly divides the many categories and specializations in DeFi, and the separated sectors help you track the project that you believe offers the highest profits.

DeFi Prime allows you to track the AMM that is best for your yield farming methods and meets your idea of what a yield aggregator should be in the case of yield aggregators. From Pickle, a platform that allows you to maximize your returns while avoiding the hassles of yield farming, to BeefyFinance, a cross-chain yield optimizer, the list is extensive and a must-know for DeFi enthusiasts. Finally, DeFi prime allows you to watch DeFi platforms by displaying a list of projects and their associated interest rates, making decisions, and following where the best earnings are.

Yield Farming Binance Smart Chain Tool

Yield Watch

On the Binance Smart Chain, yield watch is perhaps the oldest yield farming tool. Initially, the yields tracking dashboard was only accessible for Pancakeswap, but it is now available for several AMMs, including BeefyFinance and ApeSwap. Yield watch is a DeFi dashboard that allows you to track the success of your yield farming, lending, and liquidity pool. Furthermore, the application is mobile-friendly and allows you to see all of your LP staked in different AMM's with associated APYs and possible temporary losses, among other things, at a glance.

The DeFi dashboard now provides a premium option that allows users to track $200 in LP tokens for every $1 in $WATCH they have. Different base currencies, an individual TX overview, and your wallet balance shown in real-time value, among other things, are included in the pro service. Yield watch is the right choice for you if you're an active user of the BSC and are looking for a yield farming tool tailored for usage on the chain. The UI is basic and straightforward whether you're a newbie or an expert in DeFi.

Yield Farming Ethereum Tools

Yield Farming Tools

Yield farming tools display the APR of prominent Ethereum pools (such as Curve) in several time intervals, including hourly, daily, and weekly. It also assists you in determining if the benefits outweigh the risks and deciding on the DeFi protocol based on the risk/reward ratio idea. Yield farming tools are great for everyday Ethereum Blockchain users since it also displays the gas fee to help you decide whether delivering LPs is worth the gas fees and a tool to calculate the impermanent loss. You have complete control over the price fluctuations for both sets of token pairings, and the yield tracking dashboard shows you the precise percent of temporary losses.

Yield Farming Polygon Tools

Cryptonuts

Cryptonuts is likely the only yield farming tool that supports Polygon. It covers many AMMs, allowing you to track many farms, track their APR, and compare it to the TVL to see if the Dex is famous among DeFi enthusiasts. Additionally, Cryptonuts allows you to follow your staked amounts by linking your wallet to the site, and it has a complete assessment of each AMM listed on its site, so be sure to check it out when doing your research.

Yield Farming Tax Calculator

Tax Calculator

How to monitor the amount earned through taxable yield farming is a commonly asked question in DeFi. This is where Tax Calculator comes in, emphasizing accuracy and a dependable platform. The Tax Calculator is an excellent tool for both investors and accountants. The Tax tool, which prioritizes accuracy and ease of use, also allows trading on all major DeFi and Dex platforms, including UniSwap. Unlike other programs, it also includes yield farming and LP products, and to get started, simply choose the exchange and enter your wallet address.

Step-by-Step Guide to Yield Farming

Step 1

Go to the platform you'd want to use to yield your farm and scroll down until you locate the portion of the page where the various pools are mentioned, each of which will give you their yield percentages. Depending on the platform's possibilities, they can be stablecoin pools or Ethereum pools, and we will use Sushiswap as an example in this case.

Step 2

Log in to your cryptocurrency wallet, pick the number of coins you want to contribute, and select the deposit option.

Step 3

Verify that the transaction gets approved on your bitcoin wallet. This will usually appear as a pop-up window in your browser, displaying the gas fees connected with the trade. Select "Confirm" from the drop-down menu.

Step 4

Add liquidity to the liquidity pool you want to invest in and authorize the transaction on the platform.

This method may vary somewhat from one platform to the next, but it works the same way.

DeFi Yield Farming Platform to Invest in 2022

If you're serious about getting into yield farming, you'll need to know which platform to use. Let's look at the top platforms worth your time in 2022.

PancakeSwap

PancakeSwap (CAKE) is a decentralized exchange based on the Binance Smart Chain launched in 2020. PancakeSwap features several yield farms, requiring you to bet two tokens to receive the LP tokens for that farm. You can receive incentives in the form of CAKE tokens by using the LP tokens you earn by depositing tokens into your liquidity pool.

Uniswap

Uniswap is a decentralized cryptocurrency exchange and DeFi platform that allows users to earn interest on their bitcoin holdings through its liquidity pools. It's built on Ethereum and allows users to trade ERC-20 tokens. Because it is Ethereum-based, its gas prices might be significant, but it does not require any identity verification or sign-ups to use the program.

Curve Finance

Curve Finance is a decentralized exchange based on the Ethereum blockchain to facilitate fast trading between cryptocurrencies of a similar value while offering high yearly interest rates on any cryptocurrency assets placed by liquidity providers. On the Curve Finance website, some columns will show you the various APYs you may earn by supplying liquidity to each pool and the assets you will receive in return, if you receive any.

Aave

Aave is a cryptocurrency-based lending technology that lets users earn interest on their deposits while also borrowing assets. Users may deposit stablecoins into Aave and get a payout of 4.78 percent to 13.49 percent, which can add to their existing profits in the form of staked AAVE. Developers can customize the DeFi lending pool because it is open-source.

SushiSwap

SushiSwap is a DEX platform that enables participants to swap bitcoin tokens using the AMM mechanism; liquidity providers get SushiSwap Liquidity Pool Tokens (SLP tokens). Swapping, liquidity pools, staking, and other sushi-related rewards are also available. If you give liquidity, some of these platforms provide the finest yield farming, and you may employ any of them. Remember to check the TVL on each platform so you can figure out how to earn the most interest and ensure that the DeFi platforms you're about to invest in are secure.

Yield Farming Crypto Platforms for 2022 and Beyond

Aqru - Best Overall Yielding Crypto Platform for 2022

If you're seeking the finest option to make interest on your idle digital currency assets, Aqru stands out among the competition. When you register an account with this service, you will be able to earn a 7%

annual percentage yield on Bitcoin and Ethereum. This is one of the best interest rates available on these popular crypto assets.

Furthermore, unlike other yield farming crypto services, Aqru allows you to earn the above-mentioned high yield without keeping your tokens locked up for an extended period. Aqru, on the other hand, offers flexible accounts that allow you to request a withdrawal at any moment. Aqru crypto interest accounts support a variety of stablecoins and Bitcoin and Ethereum. USDC and Tether, for example, pay a 12-percent annual percentage yield. Because it provides crypto loans to retail and institutional borrowers using your deposited cash, Aqru can offer decent rates of return. Another feature you will enjoy about Aqru is that it accepts deposits in fiat currencies. This implies that even if you don't have any digital tokens, you may start receiving income on crypto. Furthermore, Aqru provides a mobile crypto app for Android and iOS phones, allowing you to access your account while on the go.

Features

- Bitcoin/Ethereum is available at a 7 percent annual percentage rate (APR).
- Stablecoins have a 12-percent APY.
- There is no lock-up period.
- Excellent reputation

eToro — A Regulated Platform that Provides Crypto Interest Tools

If safety is your first consideration while looking for the finest yield farming crypto sites, eToro is the place to go. eToro, controlled by the SEC, ASIC, FCA, and CySEC, does not provide traditional yield farming services but allows you to earn passive income. You can do this through an automated staking tool that pays out for as long as you keep the tokens in your eToro account. eToro currently supports crypto staking on Cardano, Ethereum, and Tron. There is no requirement to stake your coins for a minimum number of days as you get eToro interest-bearing tools flexibly. This is ideal for those who require immediate access to their crypto assets. eToro has low-cost brokerage and exchange services, solid regulatory status, and institutional-grade security tools.

For example, eToro allows you to buy cryptocurrency with no spread for as little as $10. Furthermore, there are no fees for depositing funds in US dollars or storing your tokens in the eToro crypto wallet. The provider's cryptocurrency wallet application allows you to exchange tokens across 500+ pairs, making eToro a popular choice for mobile users. Finally, eToro provides a copy trading service that will enable you to trade cryptocurrencies while remaining completely passive.

Features

- Regulated by the ASIC, SEC, FCA, and CySEC
- Earn interest on supported tokens automatically.
- You can withdraw your tokens at any point in time.
- Spread-only crypto buying and copy trading tools are also supported.

Crypto.com — Excellent Platform for Earning a High APY on Stablecoins

Consider Crypto.com if you want to make the greatest interest rate on cryptocurrency without worrying about price fluctuations. When you deposit stablecoins like Tether and USDC into your account with this top-rated service, you may earn an APY of 14%. Several factors will influence the actual APY you get.

For example, to earn the full 14 percent APR on Tether, you must keep your tokens locked up for three months. You'll also need to put down a minimum of 40,000 CRO tokens. However, if you deposit Tether without staking any CRO tokens and have a flexible withdrawal schedule, the APY reduces to 6%. As a result, Crypto.com provides different APYs to meet various needs.

With that stated, Crypto.com provides over 250 digital currencies that pay interest, most of which are not stablecoins. This encompasses everything from Bitcoin, Ethereum, and Litecoin to Solana, Shiba Inu, and Decentraland. The lock-up time and whether or not you choose to stake CRO tokens determines the APY you can earn. Crypto.com, nevertheless, has a popular mobile app that allows you to access your account no matter where you are.

Features

- More than 250 coins are supported.
- Appealing interest rates
- Stake CRO tokens to increase APYs.

BlockFi – A Popular Bitcoin Yields Platform

BlockFi, one of the best cryptocurrency exchanges, provides several cryptocurrency-related services. The platform offers acceptable APYs on stablecoins and traditional digital assets to earn interest. When you deposit Tether in your BlockFi account, you may earn an APY of 9.25 percent on the former. And, without a lock-up period, this rate is paid up to the first 20,000 USDT deposited. The highest rate on offer is 4.5 percent if you're searching for a return on your Bitcoin investments. This rate applies to the first 0.10 BTC of your deposit. Following that, the rate reduces to 1%. Ethereum offers a little better deal at 5%, although this only applies to the first 1.5 percent of ETH. BlockFi stores most digital client money in cold storage for security reasons. Furthermore, significant third-party exchanges, like Gemini, hold digital tokens.

BlockFi also has the policy to protect itself against a remote hack. BlockFi offers standard trading accounts in addition to crypto yield services. This allows you to purchase and trade digital currencies at a reasonable cost. As a result, once you've acquired a crypto asset on the BlockFi platform, you may immediately begin earning returns. BlockFi is excellent at providing excellent customer service, including phone assistance.

Features

- Specialist crypto-interest earning site
- A wide variety of tokens are supported
- There are no lock-up periods
- Stablecoins have the best rates.

Coinbase — Best Yield-Generating Platform for Newbies

Coinbase is among the largest cryptocurrency exchanges in terms of user accounts, with tens of millions of traders using the site. You may quickly purchase digital currencies with a debit or credit card, and the Coinbase trading platform is ideal for newcomers. You may start collecting interest after you have cryptocurrency in your Coinbase account.

This is made possible via the company's automatic staking mechanism, which has no lock-up time. Coinbase only offers six tokens because it is a newcomer to the crypto dividend field. This comprises Cosmos (5%), Tezos (4.63%), Ethereum (4.5%), and Algorand (4.5%). Dai (2%), and USDC (1%), are examples of stablecoins. Although Coinbase is great for beginners, the APYs aren't as good as those offered by competing platforms. Coinbase has some of the industry's greatest security mechanisms, including cold storage, two-factor authentication, and IP address/device whitelisting. Furthermore, Coinbase is not only a regulated organization in the United States, but it also trades on the NASDAQ. Coinbase is also a fantastic choice to build a diverse cryptocurrency portfolio, as the site offers over 50 different digital assets.

Features

- The regulated entity is in the US

- Withdrawals are not subject to any penalties.
- You can deposit funds in either cryptocurrency or US dollars.
- Beginners will love it.

2022 Yield Farming Opportunities

We're seeing an ever-growing trend of users being able to partake in the upside of a protocol's growth as we continue to observe the rise of a fascinating new financial industry. DeFi is unleashing a set of new and intriguing passive income options, whether as basic as lending cryptocurrency on Compound or something more advanced like engaging in liquidation auctions on Maker.

CRV Liquidity Mining Curve

- Platforms Used: Curve, Synthetix, Ren Protocol, yEarn
- Utilize the Curve DAO and a range of Curve liquidity metrics to increase your CRV profits.
- You can place collateral in any of Curve's liquidity pools.
- If you want to join a Bitcoin pool, utilize Ren Protocol to convert BTC to Ethereum.
- Use a Curve gauge to stake your liquidity token.
- Claim CRV and lock it using the Curve DAO for a multiplier on your liquidity.

Watch out for more SNX and REN bonuses for the sUSD and sBTC pools.

Compound COMP Yield Farming

- Platforms Used: Maker, Compound, Curve & InstaDapp
- Increase the value of your COMP holdings by using stablecoin leverage to push composability to its limit.
- To establish a vault and receive DAI, deposit ETH using Oasis Borrow (Maker).
- Open an InstaDapp DeFi Smart Account and deposit DAI.

- Transfer freshly deposited Dai to InstaDapp's Compound section.
- To take a leveraged DAI position against your DAI holdings, use InstaDapp's "Maximize COMP Earnings" tool.
- Supply DAI directly on Compound as an alternative.
- You can be liquidated if your collateralization falls short of the minimum amount when employing the InstaDapp technique. When adopting this method, we recommend keeping to a 60 percent ratio.

SushiSwap SUSHI Liquidity Mining

- Platforms Used: SushiSwap
- You may earn SUSHI governance tokens by supplying liquidity to any of SushiSwap's incentivized liquidity pools.
- Go to SushiSwap's Menu of the Week to see which pools are incentivized
- Connect your sushi.com wallet to any of the approved pools to provide liquidity.
- To begin receiving rewards, stake LP tokens in the appropriate pool on SushiSwap.

Curve Bitcoin Yield Farming

- Platforms Used: Ren Protocol, Curve, Synthetix, Balancer
- Depositing tokens into a Yearn Vault will earn you yield.
- To get yCurve, deposit liquidity into Curve's Y Pool.
- It stakes yCurve on yEarn by using the Vault interface.

Curve Bitcoin Yield Farming

- Platforms Used: Ren Protocol, Curve, Synthetix, Balancer
- For supplying liquidity to the sBTC Curvepool, you can earn SNX, REN, BAL, and CRV.

- Using the Ren Bridge, convert Bitcoin to Ethereum.
- sBTC Curvepool is where you should deposit your freshly earned renBTC.
- Stake your ySBTC tokens in the LP Rewards area of Mintr.
- Receive SNX/REN Balancer Pool Tokens as a prize.
- Balancer allows you to withdraw SNX and REN incentives immediately.

KNC Staking Rewards Through KyberDAO

- Platforms Used: Kyber Network, Uniswap
- Stake KNC via KyberDAO and participate in protocol governance to earn ETH.
- You can purchase KNC on a DEX such as KyberSwap or Unsiwap.
- Connect your web 3 wallets like MetaMask holding KNC to the Kyber Voting Dashboard.
- KNC is deposited and used for voting.
- Vote on suggestions for each Epoch to receive a pro-rata share of ETH.
- Optional: Delegate your KNC voting authority to a Pool Master, such as the Kyber Community Pool, to vote for you.

mStable MTA Liquidity Mining

- Platforms Used: mStable, Balancer
- For supplying liquidity to the mUSD/USDC, mUSD/WETH, or mUSD/MTA Balancer Pools, earn MTA governance tokens.
- You can deposit DAI, USDC, USDT, and TUSD on mStable to create mUSD.
- To this Balancer Pool, add an equal amount of mUSD and USDC.
- Alternative: Invest in mUSD with mStable Save to earn a competitive APY in mUSD.

Synthetix sUSD Liquidity Incentives

- Platforms Used: iEarn & Mintr (Synthetix)
- Earn weekly SNX inflation as a reward for supplying liquidity to the sUSD Curvepool using iEarn and Curve.

Uniswap Liquidity Provider Tutorial

- Platforms Used: Uniswap, Zapper
- By providing liquidity, divide 50 percent between ETH and 50 percent between the target ERC20 Token, you may earn a part of Uniswap's 0.3 percent trading fees on any ERC20 token pair.
- USD Liquidity Incentives Synthetix
- It uses iEarn and Mintr as platforms (Synthetix)
- Earn weekly SNX inflation as a reward for supplying liquidity to the sUSD Curvepool using iEarn and Curve.

CHAPTER 4

DEFI LENDING AND BORROWING IN 2022

Basics

Until recently, safe lending and borrowing were exclusive to banks and other established financial organizations until recently. People go to their bank when they need a loan, mortgage, or credit, and they go to the same bank, an adviser, or other traditional financial services when they wish to invest their money. This process was the standard for decades, and it instills a great deal of faith in these characters to do the right thing.

DeFi does not imply dismantling the existing financial system. DeFi, however, imitates and enhances traditional finance. Many projects try to deliver standard banking capabilities in a unique method that protects users from interacting with centralized intermediaries such as banks.

Borrowing and lending are difficult to envision in the global financial system, which is true in the decentralized financial system. DeFi has created innovative ways to allow users to borrow and lend crypto assets over the last year, successfully launching shared, public, and decentralized lending platforms in the blockchain ecosystem. Decentralized lending and borrowing appear similar to traditional finance: you may borrow money or invest it to earn investment interest.

While the ultimate aim seems to be the same, the methods used to get there are primarily different.

DeFi borrowers and lenders have a simple relationship, lenders supply cash in exchange for interest, and borrowers pay interest to use those funds. Each transaction appears to be similar to any other loan or investment, but the interaction between the two parties is unique. It's a never-ending, symbiotic arrangement in which thousands of parties borrow and lend from one other without ever having to engage personally. As a result, we're seeing the emergence of autonomous, decentralized money markets.

How DeFi Lending Works

DeFi lending, which involves a user depositing funds into a protocol, is similar to a typical cash deposit or investment that pays interest over time. Lenders receive not only interest on their digital assets but also a governance token or DAI as a bonus: Compound awards COMP, Aave generates LEND, and Maker issues DAI. The 3-5 percent interest rate for lending is better than many banks for ordinary consumers, but it may not be enough to warrant the ever-present risk of the smart contract. However, these rates look pretty appealing to high-capital investors, hedge funds, or institutions, mainly when applied to stablecoins like USDT, USDC, or DAI. Lending can also help reduce the risks of market volatility by allowing users to make money without having to trade.

Lending rates vary with each Ethereum block, for the most part, and price oracles help determine the optimal APY, which keeps the system functioning smoothly. Users who lend cryptocurrencies get platform-specific tokens (cTokens for Compound and aTokens for Aave). For example, if you deposit 1 ETH on Compound, you will receive 50 cETH tokens. The platforms use these tokens to calculate your accumulated interest and are required to redeem your funds.

How DeFi Borrowing Works

Most assets on a lending platform aren't there to earn interest. Becoming a lender is just the tip of the iceberg; the true magic emerges when considering the range of options available to lenders. However, first and foremost, it's crucial to understand the need for collateral.

The usage of decentralized protocols does not need authorization. As a result, you can not use traditional assessments such as credit score, equity, or income to calculate a safe loan amount. However, lending sites demand borrowers to use crypto assets as collateral. Over-collateralization is a common feature of DeFi loans, and this implies that consumers can only get a fraction of the collateral they have put up. You can get up to $7,500 in DAI or other assets if you lend $10,000 in ETH (approximately 75 percent of your collateral). This may sound contradictory, but it's vital to verify that every user can repay their loan. Otherwise, the system can liquidate your collateralized assets.

Compound solely provides variable interest rates for loans, whereas Aave consumers can choose between fixed and variable interest rates. Variable rates subject debtors to liquidation if the APY surpasses a particular level. These variable-rate loans need daily attention. However, depending on the current amount lent and borrowed, they are typically less expensive than fixed-rate loans.

Integrating DeFi Lending and Borrowing

Sometimes, investors borrow against their assets for a loan worth less than their collateral. This is because many crypto investors do not want to sell their most valuable assets, and they can free up liquidity without having to trade by lending their money. If someone has $50,000 in ETH and doesn't want to sell it, they can give it to a lending protocol and borrow up to 75% of its value.

This opens up a whole new universe of possibilities for crypto traders: they may undertake open market margin trading, buy a coin they don't own for liquidity mining, or take out a short-term loan for real-world crises. Hedge funds and organizations that hold cryptocurrency as part of their portfolio may find crypto lending particularly beneficial. They can take out a loan against their crypto assets and convert them to traditional financial instruments. These are only a handful of the numerous applications.

DeFi Lending Risk

Impermanent loss, DeFi rug pull strategies, and flash loan attacks are three significant DeFi lending risks. Now let's take a closer look at these risks.

Impermanent Loss

For many reasons, an impermanent loss is one of the most prevalent responses to inquiries like "What are the risks of DeFi lending?" The most significant cause of impermanent loss is the volatile nature of crypto assets. For DeFi lending, investors must lock their assets in liquidity pools, and any change in the price of the assets after placing them in the pool results in an impermanent loss. To acquire in-depth insights on DeFi risks such as an impermanent loss, you must first grasp the principles of liquidity pools in DeFi.

The AMM mechanism in popular DeFi liquidity pools significantly impacts the impermanent loss risk. With two tokens, DeFi pools must maintain a ratio of assets in the pool at a specific ratio. If you set the pool's ratio at 1:50, a liquidity pool, for example, might include both ETH and LINK tokens. As a result, everyone who wishes to provide liquidity to the pool should deposit ETH and LINK in the same ratio. The risks of impermanent loss in DeFi lending are large because DeFi pools rely heavily on arbitrage traders to match the tokens' values with market value. When the value of the tokens in the pool changes, they can add higher-value tokens to the pool. As a result, if the value of

LINK falls, arbitrage traders will add ETH to the pool in exchange for the removal of LINK.

When arbitrage traders add merely one token in excess to remove the discounted token, the coin ratio changes; as a result, the liquidity pool would automatically raise the price of the high-supply token, LINK, while lowering the cost of ETH, enticing you to rebalance the pool. After the pool rebalances, you get exposed to the DeFi risks of impermanent loss. The value of the liquidity pool has risen, but it is still less than the value of the assets in the lending protocol. The difference would provide you with a numerical representation of impermanent loss.

You may have noticed that one of the most significant risks in DeFi financing is an impermanent loss. Nevertheless, the impermanent loss should not prevent you from enjoying the full potential of DeFi lending. In reality, DeFi lending protocols reward liquidity providers with a percentage of the pool's trading costs based on their shareholding. Additional rewards may help in mitigating the impact of impermanent losses. By selecting liquidity pools with low-volatility assets, you may reduce the risk of impermanent loss associated with DeFi lending. Impermanent loss should be considered a reasonable risk rather than a roadblock in the DeFi ecosystem.

Rug Pulls by DeFi

DeFi rug is one of the most noteworthy responses to the question "what are the risks of DeFi lending" and has lately been a critical element in the DeFi space. Even if DeFi appears to be pretty promising, the ecosystem lacks a defined set of laws. As a result, investors must have faith in the platforms they are ready to lend their funds or acquire tokens. However, investors may be vulnerable to rug pull scams upon a breach of trust. DeFi developers establish a new token and combine it with other cryptocurrencies like ETH to create liquidity pools in similar frauds. The creators publicize the new coin and urge others to deposit it in the pool.

The DeFi developers employ back doors after gathering a significant sum of the top cryptocurrency, ETH, in the pool. The back doors incorporated into the token's smart contract help create millions of additional coins. Developers might sell the new coins for ETH, draining the ETH pool and leaving just the worthless tokens. The developers would then vanish, leaving no trace behind.

In 2020, one of the most well-known cases of rug pull concerns in DeFi loans received attention. SushiSwap's creator, Chef Nomi, sold his SUSHI tokens after amassing over a billion dollars in collateral. The event nearly halved the value of Uniswap's competing token. It's one of the most dramatic events in DeFi history, bringing attention to the risks of DeFi. DeFi rug pulls and exit schemes contribute to over 99 percent of all blockchain-related fraud activity in a billion-dollar market.

Flash Loan Attacks

The last answer to the question "What are the risks of lending on DeFi?" is flash loans. Flash loans are new loans that don't require collateral in the DeFi market. There are two categories of loans in the traditional banking world: unsecured and secured loans. Unsecured loans are usually for lower sums of money and do not require any form of security. Conversely, secured loans are larger and need specified protection, such as an investment, home, automobile, or different items. Banks can assess a client's reliability throughout the lending process by utilizing measures such as credit ratings and reports.

As a different type of unsecured loan based on smart contracts, flash loans are significant in DeFi lending risks. Smart contracts are used in flash loans to eliminate all risks associated with unsecured loans in traditional banking. On the contrary, flash loans have a feature distinguishing them from other loans. When taking out a flash loan, borrowers must return the entire amount borrowed in a single transaction. If the borrower defaults on the loan, the lender can reverse the transaction.

However, flash loans might pose a significant risk in DeFi lending since malevolent players can use them to manipulate the market. Specific agents might use flash loans to take advantage of the susceptible DeFi lending regulations for personal gain.

Top DeFi Lending Platforms in 2022

Choosing the right platform is crucial whether you're a borrower or a lender. Always consider the essential elements, such as interest rates, and check whether they contain the assets you wish to borrow and the level of safety and security.

The following is a list of the most popular DeFi lending platforms for asset lending.

Aave

It's a non-custodial, decentralized, open-source liquidity market protocol in which you may participate as both a lender and a borrower. It is based on Ethereum and allows users to borrow money through a simple and user-friendly interface. It generates aToken and lends as two DeFi token models. The aToken model is an ERC-20 token in which lenders' interest compounds. At the same time, LEND is a governance token in which you can receive various loans and lending services such as rate switching, uncollateralized loans, flash loans, and more.

Maker

It's a decentralized borrowing and lending platform quickly becoming one of the most outstanding DeFi lending systems. Maker is also known as the MCD (Multi-Collateral DAI) system. In smart contracts, it has more than $7 billion in tokens. MKR and DAI are the Maker's significant tokens, and both are ERC-20 tokens. Once the smart contracts are in place, DAI is linked to the dollar for lending and borrowing. DAO is an Ethereum-based decentralized lending service that supports the DAI, a stable token tied to the US dollar. It also allows users with access to ETH and MetaMask to lend in the DAI system.

Uniswap

It is among the most popular decentralized exchanges built on the Ethereum platform. It allows users to exchange between ETH and ERC-20 tokens or earn a fee by giving any amount of liquidity; consequently, you may token swap through liquidity pools. The good news is that there are presently no restrictions on Uniswap. You can exchange ERC20 tokens using a simple user interface secure, undamaged, and non-custodial. You may trade any ERC20 token on this platform or earn a fee by providing liquidity to the process. You may also either add liquidity to an existing pool or create a new one.

Unique and easily transferable ERC20 token represents every liquidity pair is represented by an. As a result, setting up a liquidity pool on Uniswap is simple; all you need is a token pair for markets. The market makers who use the standard product market maker procedure set the exchange rates.

Compound

Borrowers and lenders may use this decentralized money market technology to protect their crypto assets in the contract. It is built on the Ethereum blockchain, allowing holders of digital assets to borrow and lend crypto in exchange for security. It differs from other DeFi lending services in that it uses cookies to keep tokenization assets locked in its system. Additionally, users can add assets to their liquidity pool and earn compound interest. Compound allows users to take out over-collateralized loans, manage several assets, and be thoroughly inspected and legally confirmed. It puts aside 10% of interest payments as reserves, with the remainder to liquidity providers.

InstaDApp

It's a secure smart wallet for decentralized financial transactions. The good news is that it is a multi-purpose platform that effectively handles digital assets. InstaDApp allows users to optimize, manage, and place assets to maximize profits across various protocols. You may use this platform to receive different services, including borrowing, lending, leveraging, swapping, etc. It's similar to a bank in that it allows you to combine services to meet your needs. It offers users a user interface to manage their DeFi investments and migrate to cheaper loan platforms with lower interest rates, such as Compound, Maker, and others.

They also provide you with a DeFi protocol smart wallet portal. The most appealing aspect of InstaDApp is that it is entirely free to use; all you need is enough ETH to cover the transaction cost.

dYdX

It's an Ethereum-based non-custodial trading platform aimed at seasoned investors. It introduced margin trading, derivatives, and options to the blockchain sector, ubiquitous in currency markets and traditional investments. dYdX is a platform for lending, trading, and borrowing DAI, ETH, and USDC. It also allows users to trade cross margin and isolated margin utilizing a perpetual market contract of BTC/USDC with 10x leverage. The good news is that, unlike other DeFi lending platforms, it does not have a native token and instead charges trading fees in the supported coins.

They provide loans with a 125 percent collateral requirement and a 115 percent self-liquidation requirement. dYdX trades more than $35 million each day, making it one of the world's largest decentralized exchanges for crypto-assets and derivatives.

Popular Crypto to Collateralize DeFi Loan

Although stablecoins have shown to be the most profitable alternative for supplying cash in lending, cryptocurrency has emerged as a suitable option. Here is a list of cryptocurrencies you can use to collateralize your DeFi loan.

Ether (ETH)

Ether is Ethereum's fuel primarily utilized for payment for network transactions. As a result of the liquid nature of ETH, we've seen ETH as collateral dominate the great majority of borrowing. While ETH is still a volatile commodity, almost every lending platform accepts it. It has swiftly established itself as the most popular asset to use as collateral for a cryptocurrency-based loan.

Bitcoin (BTC)

Bitcoin is swiftly finding its way to DeFi, mainly in borrowing, because of its liquid nature. Users may post BTC as collateral and obtain stablecoins like USDC or DAI in return, thanks to services like Atomic Loans. While several token wrappers have emerged (tBTC, wBTC, pBTC, and so on), it's evident that many are aiming to profit off Bitcoin's massive market value as the leading cryptocurrency. Users are borrowing against assets with significant market capitalizations and liquid capital pools.

DeFi Lending and Borrowing Strategies

- Keep an eye on the ever-changing local crypto regulations

Recently, Crypto legislation has provoked numerous heated disputes among lawmakers, particularly in the United States. Multiple state attorney generals recently sent stop and desist orders to one popular lending platform, blockfi, right in time for its anticipated IPO. Since then, state authorities have been cracking down on all DeFi lending platforms, claiming they engage in the "selling of unregistered securities. Another platform, poly network, revealed a security compromise that cost customers $600.

Coinbase (COIN 1.82 percent), one of the world's largest decentralized exchange platforms, has revealed its intention to approach the Securities and Exchange Commission with its regulatory framework proposal. It's worth noting that this occurred only weeks after Coinbase was forced to close down its own crypto lending business due to SEC securities law breaches. Expect more significant crypto firms to accept this form of regulation on their terms as crypto's growing popularity gets further attention from regulators of all shades — or risk having governments push it upon them.

- Only use well-established lending platforms

Credible lending platforms, such as traditional banks will partner with expert suppliers to ensure your bitcoin is stored safely. Search for centralized platforms and margin lending funds, rather than DeFi platforms, to identify genuine platforms. Examine the small print to determine whether and how an exchange will secure your money against theft or other disasters. Celsius guarantees all of its customers' funds against loss with Fireblocks and Primetrust, which cover all assets stored on the Celsius platform and wallet. Keep in mind that this insurance does not cover any losses incurred due to borrowed funds, such as a hacker gaining access to your wallet.

Crypto.com also has excellent crypto insurance coverage through a Lloyd's of London branch. It will cover up to $750 million in total losses throughout the exchange, including third-party theft; however, we don't know if this will cover every holding on Crypto.com because the firm doesn't publish its total assets. Nonetheless, that level of security dramatically increases the safety of your assets.

- Borrow, lend, and get your interest paid in stablecoins or fiat currency

Ethereum (ETH 2.14 percent) and Cardano (ADA 1.37 percent) are volatile altcoins. Because they're linked to the borrower, you won't be able to sell them and reduce your losses if they decline while you're lending them out. On the flip side, an altcoin you're presently lending may experience substantial increases, which would be suitable for borrowers but bad for you. The same goes for interest; if you get paid in altcoins for lending, the value of the coins can plummet the next day.

Stablecoins, conversely, are backed by either the US dollar or gold. Whatever happens in the crypto world, they'll always be set to resist volatility. The most well-known stablecoins are Tether (USDT 0.00 percent), USD Coin (USDC -0.02 percent), and Binance USD, all tied 1:1 to the US dollar.

If you insist on lending out altcoins, you won't miss out on any gains if the value of the coin you're lending out rises dramatically. Look for reliable platforms that allow automatic price modifications; if the value of the crypto you loan grows while you're lending it, the amount the borrower must repay rises. This prevents borrowers from collecting profits not written into their loans, but it also provides you, the lender, with earnings that you may keep or use toward your next investment. When it comes to interest, being paid in stablecoins protects your rewards for lending out your coins first while also allowing you to sell those stablecoins for a growing cryptocurrency the next time you see it heading upward.

- Unless you're a seasoned crypto trader, steer clear of DeFi platforms

If your bank goes bankrupt, the government will reimburse you up to $100,000 per account. However, if you lose all of your assets in an unforeseen way on a DeFi platform, you have no one to blame but yourself. Users can borrow digital money using decentralized finance platforms like Compound or Aave or centralized finance (CeFi) networks like Celsius. All DeFi loan services use a blockchain to log their transactions; no traditional bank or other central authority is involved. While it's convenient not to entrust your assets to a third party, DeFi protocols are vulnerable to technical attacks and hackers.

However, on any centralized finance network, the company's owners serve as the central authority. As a result, as a lender, you must have complete assurance that whoever runs the platform is acting in good faith. Check whether any centralized finance platform you're considering has a recovery structure, such as a custody firm that protects your funds if your assets are hacked or lost.

Joining a margin lending fund like Invictus capital is a more mainstream and reputable way to become a crypto lending investor. Invictus provides a seamless service that allows lenders to earn from the crypto assets in their portfolios. In a custody account, your money is managed by a big financial institution, such as Citigroup, which must follow strict custody requirements and provide you with monthly statements detailing your accounts. These funds will not compensate you if your investments lose value in the market, but they will protect you if the currency's inventors commit fraud and flee with your money.

CHAPTER 5

BUILDING DEFI PROJECTS IN 2022

B uilding an excellent DeFi project needs a wide range of talents and experience in the industry. To create a DeFi project, the owner must consider several unique market characteristics and fundamentals. The following are the main aspects you should be aware of to develop a successful DeFi project:

- Time to complete a project
- Integration with a different DeFi
- Dedicated community
- Analysis of business logic
- Experienced DeFi developer

Time to Complete a Project

The DeFi ecosystem is evolving at a tremendous speed. One of the key objectives is to give a novel or superior solution in a reasonable amount of time. Based on an average estimation, four months is optimal for DeFi project development. However, it's important to divide this time intelligently into three main categories:

- Planning phase
- Development phase
- Testing phase

Surprisingly, the first and third phases should take a large part of your time. Therefore, you must prioritize architectural project planning and project testing.

Integration with a DeFi

Your DeFi app will not exist in a vacuum, and therefore it won't be the "only" one on the market; thus, it will have to interact with other DeFi projects. DeFi is evolving into a broad, ramified, and integrated ecosystem in which its projects compete or are linked to one another. yEarn is a well-known aggregator project that connects to many other DeFis and allows its customers to gain more from such collaboration. In most cases, early integration should begin with partnerships with market leaders such as Curve.fi, Compound, Balancer, or Aave. However, before implementing the code, this stage necessitates much investigation.

These protocols have distinct interfaces and features that may be critical for integration. As a result, your developers should have extensive writing and understanding of code expertise. The challenge of bringing many DeFi protocols together in your own app's unified interface isn't easy, and it often necessitates unique solutions and expertise. Despite the great difficulty, it provides versatility since it allows you to design various DeFi strategies and swap between them. As a result, your protocol will generate more profit.

Dedicated Community

Investigate the community interested in your decentralized project ideas and catch up with them. Users of your project are always willing to give suggestions about improving their experience with it, and you can find these ideas or proposals in Telegram or Twitter groups. Please make an effort to stay in touch with the community and pay attention to their suggestions and opinions. It will undoubtedly assist you in meeting the particular needs of your participants and preventing liquidity migration out of your protocol.

Analysis of Logic

A business analysis of your idea is essential for building a DeFi project. Many projects fail not because they are bad or have a shoddy tech stack but rather because of a lack of comprehensive business analysis. Remember not to start architecture development without a carefully prepared SRS with complete requirements. Your DeFi project will have a higher chance of success if you do this: In your project's SRS, you must analyze the definition and execution stages thoroughly. Make sure you include them in your business analysis.

Experienced DeFi Developers

The DeFi project development necessitates diverse skills and a deeper understanding of financial and blockchain technology. To create a decentralized financial project, you will need an experienced team of developers. Below are the most important developers team considerations to make throughout the project development:

- Development of Smart Contracts
- Project Testing
- DAO
- UI/UX

Development of Smart Contracts

Smart contracts are the foundation of every DeFi project or decentralized peer-to-peer trading. They frequently represent sophisticated and extensive codes in open finance, encrypting a wide range of protocol functions. A smart contract must cover all conceivable processes and activities the user might do. At the same time, everything should be clear and secure, which adds to the initial contract's complexity. The contract's trustworthiness is the next consideration;

you must effectively protect it from hackers because it involves large sums of money.

As previously said, creating a DeFi project nowadays necessitates integration with other DeFis. So, in this case, the issue is the complexity of the various protocols you'd like to incorporate. Hence, developers must thoroughly examine and understand this code to ensure a secure and dependable integration. Otherwise, when swiping between two or more protocols, the money can be stolen or trapped in a smart contract. This adds to the development difficulty and necessitates using an experienced team of developers with an excellent understanding of solidity.

Testing of The Project

Unit tests and security audits are essential for your contracts to function correctly. They are, however, double-checking the formal logic and mainly focusing on the smart contracts section of the project.

DAO

The project must have its governance token. The functionality of a token is one of the most important aspects to consider. Functionality is used within the network and your community to govern the protocol and receive the rewards. This will attract users in two ways: first, monetization, and second, engagement. The capitalization of a token will rise due to its use; therefore, being rewarded in your governance token will result in actual money. Second, users will be able to utilize this token, for instance, in DAO, to vote on protocol upgrades. As a result, tokenizing a protocol and keeping the community engaged in protocol administration and enhancement benefit your DeFi project.

User Interface/User Experience (UI/UX) Design

UI/UX design is equally crucial when creating a decentralized financial project. It's preferable if an outsourcing business can provide a comprehensive solution, with one team working on your project from start to finish. To make your DeFi app's user experience fluid, prioritize user profit metrics. Consider placing an APY index at the top of the main page or in another clear location.

DeFi Protocols to use in 2022

DeFi protocols are designed for various applications in the financial sector, particularly borrowing and lending. At the same time, it's worth noting that the DeFi ecosystem is still in its early stages, and many of the projects carry significant risks. Nevertheless, we have prepared a list of notable and excellent DeFi projects for different investment activities in the DeFi ecosystem.

Aave

Aave is among the most popular and prominent lending protocols in the DeFi ecosystem. It uses the native token AAVE to secure the protocol while also allowing users to participate in its governance. Users can earn AAVE incentives by staking AAVE tokens in the Safety Module. Review more about this protocol in the earlier chapters.

yEarn

yEarn is another standout among the most excellent DeFi protocols. It's essentially a fully automated liquidity aggregator with a range of yield farming possibilities. The yEarn native coin, YFI, is in charge of the protocol's governance. Users could stake YFI tokens in exchange for a pro-rata portion of protocol fees and participation in the protocol's governance.

Synthetix

Synthetix is the next significant addition among the top DeFi protocols on this list. It is among the most well-known derivatives protocols, and it has its native coin, SNX. With SNX tokens, users must invest at least

750 percent of the value of new derivatives to be produced, known as Synths.

Compound

It is the most widely used loan protocol. COMP is a native token that users may earn by lending or borrowing assets on the platform. The Compound Governance Dashboard, which allows for voting and delegation, is also useful for governing crucial protocol choices.

Uniswap

Uniswap is another excellent DeFi protocol. In the DeFi ecosystem, it is now the most popular decentralized exchange. Users may earn UNI, the native cryptocurrency, by providing liquidity to specific pools.

Kyber Network

Another potential example among major decentralized exchanges, or DEXs, is the Kyber Network. Kyber Network Crystals, or KNC, are the native tokens on Kyber Network. Users may use their KNC tokens to get the power to vote and delegate on important choices like the implementation of essential governance systems.

Sushiswap

Sushiswap is a loan and automated market maker (AMM) system featuring the SUSHI governance token. LP can earn the SUSHI token by providing liquidity to selected pairings on Sushiswap. You use the Omaske bar to collect protocol fees and issue protocols, allowing users to stake SUSHI tokens.

Maker

Maker would undoubtedly be the next most important addition to the DeFi protocols list. Maker is one of the most well-known decentralized lending systems. The Maker DeFi protocol's significance in creating

DAI is a standout feature. Maker's native token, MKR, may be used to vote on protocol choices via the Maker voting dashboard.

Balancer

Balancer is also one of the few DeFi protocols that recently received substantial attention. The Balancer DeFi system focuses on automated asset management and liquidity, with the added benefit of native token governance. BAL, the native token, aids in controlling critical protocol elements, including support assets and protocol fees.

Numerai

Numerai is yet another well-known DeFi protocol on the market. It's an AI-powered hedge fund that developed the erasure protocol, which can aid in forecasting. Users might use their NMR token stakes in the prediction system to demonstrate their trust in the forecasts.

Project Serum

Project Serum is also one of the most popular DeFi protocols today, and it is the newest addition to decentralized exchanges or DEXs. Project Serum's distinguishing features include that it is permissionless and not built on the Ethereum network.

Index Cooperative

The Index Cooperative is a non-profit organization that works to improve the DeFi Pulse Index, or DPI, based on the DeFi protocol and acts as an index management mechanism. The native INDEX governance token aids in the determination of index content, and it also aids in figuring out how to use the indexes in meta-governance for connected protocols.

Curve

Curve is a notable and excellent DeFi protocol, and it functions as a liquidity aggregator for assets with the same peg as Bitcoin wraps and stablecoins. The Curve DAO allows users to stake the curve protocol's native currency, CRV, to achieve efficient time-weighted governance. In addition, CRV liquidity mining can earn users' liquidity multipliers.

0x Protocol

The 0x Protocol is also on the list of the greatest DeFi protocols because of its unique characteristics. It's a DeFi liquidity protocol that can help transfer money across different exchanges. The protocol's native coin, ZRX, might aid users in its governance, and market Makers can also stake ZRX to get trading fees.

Ren Protocol

Ren Protocol is a DeFi protocol that is also in use today. It acts as a cross-platform interface for transferring assets to Ethereum. Users can join the network as validators by putting up 100,000 REN as collateral for hosting a dark node.

Marketing Your DeFi Project

DeFi project must adopt strategies and techniques that may help them make the most of their overall marketing in an industry that is now completely saturated with both established and growing crypto enterprises. Below are some of the most effective marketing strategies currently used by many DeFi emerging enterprises.

Search Engine Optimization and Content Marketing

There is a lot to be gained by having your project online, and DeFi projects are no different. Optimizing your website and posting compelling content about your project is essential if you have long-term objectives. Otherwise, you won't be seen on search engines since you won't rank high on users' searches. The primary goal is to build a community and provide sufficient content for investors to be informed about your project and make favorable decisions regarding your business. You should regularly review and comprehend the statistics to determine which keywords and subjects are popular among your target audience. You'll know how to effectively express the project's USP (unique selling point) using keywords to attract a larger audience.

Social Media Engagement

Building an excellent community that allows for social interaction, engagement, and support is the key to effective social media marketing. You may also use social media to give community members timely updates and more information about your project. Sharing "how-to" information on your social media accounts won't be enough. You'll need to develop a strong communication strategy, create memes, and distribute engaging content with your target audience.

Twitter is one platform where crypto users are engaged, active, and interested in DeFi. The primary goal of Twitter is to grow the number of followers and level of interaction around the project organically. If you want to obtain many followers, don't waste money on Twitter ads; a well-executed Airdrop will bring people to your project. Make sure you have a staff maintaining your Twitter, Telegram, Discord, Facebook, and Reddit profiles. You may even try out other social media platforms like TikTok, which have less competition for the crypto audience.

It's OK to mix your marketing videos between the TikTok dancing challenges and humorous pranks. Users will show interest in your project if you do it correctly, helping you to get new and engaged followers. Community management has evolved as well, and it is no longer sufficient just to start a topic and provide corporate news. Make sure you watch comments 24 hours a day, seven days a week, and respond to all questions and concerns in an AMA-style way.

Influencer Marketing

By using influencers in their marketing or promotion activities, DeFi projects may profit from increased traffic and brand exposure. DeFi ventures can reach a wider targeted audience by partnering with influencers who already have a following interested in blockchain and cryptocurrency. However, because the number of fraudsters who use bots on their channels is relatively large, you should be extremely cautious while working with influencers. It will help if you collaborate with someone specializing in crypto marketing. You may also want to investigate your influencer's brand and whether it aligns with your company's profile and goal. The influencer can talk about something intriguing, which increases audience engagement. Your project, on the other side, will acquire desired exposure.

Many customers are getting more adept at recognizing sponsored influencer ads and can quickly detect a business or influencer that appears to be deceitful. Pay attention to ads performance statistics to see which influencers your target audience responds to the most.

DeFi Trackers, Ratings, and Listings

Another way to promote DeFi projects is to get them mentioned on sites dedicated to them, such as trackers, calendars, lists, and ratings. The following are the most common trackers:

- DeFipulse
- DeFiprime
- DeFi
- DeFiscore
- DeFirate

When developing a company profile, it is sensible to include data that may interest your target audience (e.g., links to GitHub code, technical documentation, press portraits of team leaders, project mission, partners, etc.). Furthermore, brand mentions on popular media sites can help enhance SEO and drive traffic to your project page. The goal is to be referenced in media content on Google's initial pages (e.g., top 10 DeFi companies, best DeFi tokens, top-yield farming projects, etc.).

PR Marketing

Collaboration with a reputable agency with a long relationship with media organizations is ideal for getting your content published on tier 1 and tier 2 media without being labeled as "sponsored." By providing DeFi projects expert aid and an understanding of the sector, crypto marketing services alleviate the burden of developing great content and building a unique brand. As a result, it's always a good idea to delegate content creation to an agency so that you can focus on other elements of your business.

If you're going to submit an article to a popular media outlet, make sure it's high-quality and valuable to the reader. That implies that rather than merely introducing readers to your project and its aims, the story itself should be committed to resolving particular problems through extensive market research. Positive media attention might help your project gain a following without spending a lot of money on promotion.

Promo, Giveaways, and Airdrops

All of these are crucial marketing methods. Despite being expensive, airdrops are an excellent method to get people interested in a project. For example, Uniswap's airdrop set a new record for the largest crypto giveaway ever and was hugely successful. Said, a DeFi enterprise may expand the presence of this token in the real world for the "price" of distributing several free tokens to investors. On the other hand, promotional efforts are not restricted to gifts and airdrops. You may create contests and games and engage your current audience in your project.

CHAPTER 6

DEFI ASSET MANAGEMENT TOOLS

Basics

DeFi asset management has always been a difficult task. It all started when the business was still in its infancy when DeFi assets were scarce. Until the first tracking applications were on the market, most traders tracked their portfolios manually. However, as the world of decentralized finance grew, so did the number of investing and portfolio alternatives. While DeFi protocols were interoperable and thus subject to community solutions, technology was suddenly not where it needed to be. DeFi portfolio trackers tried to catch up, but because most were derived from centralized finance technology, they've always been insufficient for decentralized finance.

Problems with the current app became increasingly evident as DeFi grew exponentially. Users discovered that many programs were built for desktop use and then converted for mobile use, resulting in clumsy coding and bad user experiences. Many apps were developed for use in the centralized financial area, making them inappropriate in the fast-paced decentralized finance ecosystem. There is the need for a smartphone app created from the bottom up as a portfolio tracker exclusively for DeFi on the market. Now let's delve into DeFi asset management tools categories and their examples.

DeFi Portfolio Tracker

MetaMask

One of the most widely used DeFi tools is MetaMask. Metamask is a powerful tool because it allows users to engage with the whole Ethereum ecosystem and its numerous decentralized applications, despite being a cryptocurrency wallet that runs as a browser plugin (Dapps). The wallet works with all of the most common web browsers (Chrome, Brave, Firefox, and Microsoft Edge). The Ethereum blockchain is supported, and ERC-721 tokens are utilized for NFTs.

MetaMask makes connecting to numerous decentralized crypto exchanges (DEXs) easy for DeFi users, making it a crucial DeFi tool for interoperability across different DeFi platforms.

DeFi Pulse

All DeFi applications are ranked on DeFi Pulse, which is a scoreboard. This excellent tool can assist you in keeping track of all your DeFi assets and projects. Crypto enthusiasts may also use DeFi Pulse to acquire the most up-to-date rankings and data on most DeFi protocols. In addition to other importance, it monitors the TVL of key DeFi platforms. Another valuable element of DeFi Pulse is the DeFi List, a collection of the greatest DeFi sites.

DeFi Llama

DeFi Llama is a convenient tool for tracking DeFi protocols and giving information such as TVL and changes over time. This DeFi tool seeks to catalog all DeFi protocols now available on the market, and it currently includes Ethereum, Binance Smart Chain (BSC), Solana, Avalanche, Polygon, and more platforms. DeFi Llama also makes it easy to evaluate protocols by categorizing them:

- Airdrops
- DEXs

- Assets
- Lending
- Yield
- Insurance
- Options
- Staking

DeFi Llama is a powerful DeFi tool that makes it simple for users to track and compare protocols across many blockchains.

DappRadar

DappRadar is a portal that gives data on over 3,000 different Dapps. The firm, located in Lithuania, intends to grow and incorporate as many DeFi components as possible. DappRadar's key benefit is that it makes data analysis easier for consumers and developers. Users can make better and more informed decisions by examining all accessible data regarding Dapps. DappRadar is a DeFi tool that allows developers to investigate and find new Dapps, while users may access their data and become consumers.

Coinbase Wallet

Coinbase Wallet is not confused with Coinbase, the prominent bitcoin exchange. Users may safely store and trade crypto cash and assets directly on their smartphones using Coinbase Wallet, which does not require a Coinbase account. Users may even earn interest on their crypto assets using the wallet. Unlike Coinbase, the user has total control over the wallet and access to the private keys with Coinbase Wallet. It connects Ethereum-based Dapps, such as decentralized exchanges and other DeFi services, to the Ethereum blockchain.

DeFi Saver

DeFi Saver is a simple dashboard that allows users to keep track of their money. This DeFi application makes it easy for inventors to handle all elements of their DeFi investments, such as modifying lending protocols, refinancing DeFi loans, staking cash, and executing unique transactions.

The following are some of DeFi Saver's unique features:

- The ability to design unique crypto transaction recipes
- Loan shifter
- It has an easy-to-use interface for managing various platforms and assets.
- It includes a simulation module that may benefit inexperienced investors.

Zerion

Users can manage and build their whole DeFi portfolio with Zerion. DeFi indexes and DeFi blue chips are among the tools and products available on the platform. Users may trade DeFi tokens, move assets between chains, and display their NFT collections in one area. Polygon, Optimism, Arbitrum, and BSC are among the networks supported by the platform. Zerion also combines all major decentralized exchanges and Layer 2 blockchains without charging a fee. Users of the platform may manage numerous parts of their portfolio, including pools and NFTs, thanks to the user-friendly interface. NFT users may now use widgets on their iPhones or Apple Watches to see and transfer their favorite collectibles and art to friends and family.

LiquidityFolio

LiquidityFolio helps liquidity providers manage their investments in the most widely used liquidity protocols like Uniswap, Curve, Balancer, 1inch, etc. Portfolio tracking and pool research are possible with the platform, depending on certain conditions like fees and impermanent loss. Crypto investors may use this to locate the best liquidity pools for ERC-20 tokens on supported protocols and the most excellent returns.

Zapper

Zapper is a DeFi portfolio tracker with approximately $11 billion in assets under management since May 2020. The Zapper DeFi "dashboard" allows simple tracking and displaying the DeFi assets inside your portfolio, with over 200 platforms supported. An easy-to-understand interface that helps people comprehend their present crypto investments implies you'll have better control over future activities. Additionally, the Zapper website offers a learn page that uses articles and tutorials to describe and teach DeFi topics.

Orion Protocol

The Orion protocol considers itself as a crypto market entry point. The platform provides various services, making it a one-stop shop for most crypto demands. There's a lot to gain from utilizing Orion, from trading and staking to bridge services. You can use Orion on centralized and decentralized exchanges, and consumers get the best rates with no slippage. The software also includes market analysis trading features. Similarly, you have access to arbitrage options without using numerous accounts. A developer kit, an NFT aggregator, and the ORN token, which drives the entire platform, are desirable features.

Dune Analytics

Dune Analytics is used for blockchain research. To see data from a blockchain, users may quickly write custom queries. For inquiries, the tool uses SQL, and the search results are seen on the dashboard. Users can utilize query templates or develop their own. Users may extract and analyze data from Ethereum, Matic, Optimistic, and xDai for free using Dune Analytics. The visualization function is the critical aspect of this DeFi application. And the free version's only drawback is that the user may only perform three queries at a time.

APY.Vision

APY.Vision aspires to be the go-to analytics and asset management platform for liquidity pool providers and yield producers. All DeFi investors must keep meticulous records of all services and investments to earn a profit. Fortunately, this is one of the DeFi instruments that may assist you in real-time managing DeFi liquidity situations and impermanent loss. APY.Vision, unlike other tools, gives an in-depth study of your investment's entry and exit positions. It can also create statistics for comparing temporary loss against long-term income.

Pros and Cons of Selected DeFi Tools

Zerion

Pros

- In a simple, easy-to-use interface, it keeps track of the market and your portfolio.
- The design is crisp and professional.
- You can track wallet history, token investments, liquidity you've supplied across Zerion DeFi tools.
- It's free and easy to use.
- Supports a large number of protocols

Cons

- Outside of Ethereum, there is no support for tracking on other blockchains.

Zapper

Pros

- You may track and manage your portfolio in a simple, easy-to-use interface, much like Zerion.
- It categorizes and arranges your data into logical categories such as protocols, platforms, and networks.

- It features a fantastic discovery area where you can learn about new ways to provide liquidity.
- It lets you engage with protocols directly from the app, such as swapping or staking tokens in protocols.
- It supports various blockchains, including Ethereum, Binance Smart Chain, Polygon, and cross-chain bridging.

Cons

- There isn't a mobile app available.

DappRadar

Pros

- Dapps statistics are fantastic.
- Dapp Info and Stats are incredible.
- It offers a comprehensive list of coins.

Cons

- Some design elements are clumsy and difficult to scan.
- You can not post Dapps on test nets.

DeFi Llama

Pros

- Beautiful, clutter-free design.

Cons

- There is no mobile app available.

Pulse DeFi

Pros

- It offers helpful information about DeFi protocols.
- It provides a short glimpse of various crypto financing processes, allows for basic comparisons, and is handy for rapid check-ins.

Cons

- Only a small number of protocols are available.
- More L2 choices, such as Loom, and key ETH projects, such as ENS, should be represented (ideally anything that locks up value).

APY Vision

Pros

- It has a beautiful, clutter-free design.

Cons

- Only a small number of protocols are available.
- There is a lack of protocol support outside of the top brands.

DeFi Wallet

A DeFi wallet is a non-custodial wallet where your bitcoin holdings are stored. They're non-custodial, which means that only those who know the seed phrase or private key (the equivalent of a password) may access your money. Governments, for example, cannot block the account. The following are the most important considerations when selecting a DeFi wallet:

- Non-custodial
- Compatibility
- Key-based
- Accessibility

The first thing to consider when selecting a DeFi wallet is whether or not the wallet is compatible with the tokens you want to hold. Some DeFi wallets, for example, don't support Bitcoin, so if you have BTC, you won't be able to use them.

Metamask

Metamask is a non-custodial Ethereum blockchain crypto wallet and a browser plugin that allows you to access your Ethereum dApps from Google Chrome, Microsoft Edge, Firefox, Brave Browser, and other browsers. Because of its simple user interface, Metamask has become one of the most popular cryptocurrency wallets. You may keep ETH and ERC20 tokens in this wallet. It is, nevertheless, a good choice for regular transactions, but experts do not suggest it for the long-term storage of high-value assets.

My Crypto

Another popular non-custodial mobile wallet is My Crypto, available for iOS and Android. The only thing to keep in mind is that you must complete your KYC before you set up the wallet. So, if you don't want to expose your actual identity, My Crypto wallet may not be the best option.

However, let's take a look at its advantages:

- With this wallet, a DeFi developer may receive quick access to a lending platform, built-in exchange, debit card, dApps, and more.
- As a registration bonus, you'll receive $50 in native tokens.
- It's now easier to access your hardware wallet.
- After holding your tokens in the wallet, you will receive a six percent flat interest rate.

Coinbase Wallet

If we don't include the Coinbase Wallet in our list of DeFi wallets, it will be incomplete. It is one of the most excellent cryptocurrency exchanges on the market, and they provide a standalone DeFi wallet that supports a variety of DeFi protocols, including:

- Compoundfinance
- Uniswap
- CDP Maker portal

- Airswap
- NUO network

You may also transfer funds by connecting your Coinbase account to your wallet.

Argent Wallet

Because of its non-custodial approach, the Argent wallet is becoming increasingly popular. This mobile wallet will suffice if you only want to earn interest and lend money. This wallet, accessible for Android and iOS, does not need you to keep any private keys, and it has a built-in security mechanism (Argent Guardian) to keep your private key safe. Argent is likely the most user-friendly DeFi wallet for anyone with no technical understanding.

With Argent:

- You can keep DeFi assets, Ethereum, and Bitcoin in your wallet.
- It is simple to switch between two currencies.
- You'll be able to earn interest, lend assets, and use your compound procedure.
- You can save money by avoiding transaction fees.

Frontier Wallet

It's a non-custodial, all-in-one DeFi wallet that only works on mobile devices. You can follow DeFi protocols like SYNTH, DAI, and others with this wallet. Frontier has distinct features, such as a credit and debit warning, commonly known as Smart DeFi notification. The most significant advantage of this wallet is that you can add other wallets and effortlessly trade your tokens. With your DeFi coins, you may earn up to 13 percent APR on this wallet.

Reviews are not easy to come by.

As an independent author with a tiny marketing budget, I rely on readers, like you, to leave a short review on Amazon.

Even if it's just a sentence or two!

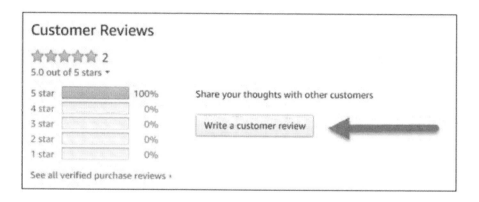

So if you enjoyed the book, please...

>> Click HERE to leave a brief review on Amazon.

I am very appreciative for your review as it truly makes a difference.

Thank you from the bottom of my heart for purchasing this book and reading it to the end.

CONCLUSION

Decentralized finance (DeFi) is undoubtedly an umbrella word for many public blockchain apps and projects to disrupt the existing finance ecosystem. DeFi has evolved into a fully functional environment of operational apps and protocols that provide value to millions of consumers. DeFi ecosystems presently hold assets worth more than $30 billion, making it one of the fastest-growing industries in the public blockchain landscape with immense profit-making opportunities.

The easiest way to make a passive income with DeFi is to deposit crypto on a site or protocol that gives an annual percentage yield. As discussed previously, another prominent way of earning from DeFi is through staking. In this process, tokens are locked inside a smart contract in return for additional tokens of the same type. Yield farming is yet another method of rewarding oneself with more of the same or a different token.

DeFi opened a new frontier for traditional finance by facilitating lending and borrowing. Decentralized lending, often known as 'Open Finance,' provided crypto holders with lending options to earn yearly returns. Individuals might borrow money at a fixed interest rate thanks to decentralized borrowing. Another popular way to make money from the DeFi space is through DeFi native activities. Many decentralized exchanges rely on liquidity pools to support trade. They provide trading liquidity to buyers and sellers in exchange for a fee. To join a pool, liquidity providers can submit specific money to a smart contract in exchange for pool tokens, generating passive profit depending on the fees traders pay when they engage with that pool.

Furthermore, yield farming, also known as liquidity mining, is another practice in the DeFi market that entails looking for a profit through different DeFi projects by engaging in liquidity pools. While yield farming is complicated, there is one primary reason why market players rush to this area: It enables you to leverage your cryptocurrency holdings to earn even more.

We are witnessing a quantum leap in the new functions of money due to distributed ledger technology innovation. Everyone is welcome to partake in the governance of DeFi projects and have a seat at the table where the world of DeFi is actively being formed. The DeFi area is progressively catching up with the traditional financial sector. Despite some of the challenges of operating on the cutting edge of innovation, the DeFi ecosystem is rising. It is difficult to forecast how this field will evolve as the ability to develop financial services becomes more democratized. However, as DeFi gains wider acceptance and more daily use cases, we will reach an inflection point in which fledgling financial technology will become a component of a new financial system that realizes the goal of a quick, safe, and accessible financial system.

Dear Reader,

As independent authors it's often difficult to gather reviews compared to much bigger publishers.

Therefore, please leave a review on the platform where you bought this book.

Many thanks,

Author Team

Want Free New Book Launches?

Email "DEFI 2022" to:

mindsetmastership@gmail.com

Made in United States
Orlando, FL
13 April 2022